CULTURES OF THE WORLD®

AZERBAIJAN

David C. King

MARSHALL CAVENDISH BENCHMARK

NEW YORK

PICTURE CREDITS
Cover: © Roger Wood/Corbis
AFP: 8, 32, 60, 61, 82, 83, 116 • ANA Press Agency: 15 • Azerbaijan International: 49, 57, 75, 76, 85,
103, 108, 117, 129 • Bes Stock: 111 • Heidi Bradner/Panos Pictures: 126 • The Bridgeman Art Library:
16, 17, 20, 55, 77, 79 • Corbis, Inc.: 3, 4, 5, 10, 14, 22, 24, 25, 27, 44, 47, 50, 54, 59, 71, 72, 74, 89, 93,
94, 96, 105, 110, 112, 113, 114, 118, 120, 123, 127, 128 • Wieland De Hoon: 18, 40, 68, 95 • Getty
Images: 1, 19, 21, 23, 28, 31, 39, 64, 70, 80, 84, 100, 102, 106, 107, 124 • HBL Network: 26, 29, 33, 42,
46, 48, 52, 65, 67, 69, 97, 101, 122 • Andy Johnstone/Panos Pictures: 109 • Krieg, Roland/Stockfood:
131 • Lehmann, Joerg/Stockfood: 130 • Lonely Planet Images: 6, 7, 43, 73, 78, 81, 88, 90, 91 • Reuters:
13, 30, 35, 36, 38, 41, 51 • Still Pictures: 58, 119, 125 • Stockfood/Gabula Art-Foto: 121 • Audrius
Tomonis/www.banknotes.com: 135 • Topfoto: 11, 12, 62, 63, 66, 99 • Travel Images: 56, 104

PRECEDING PAGE
A group of young Azerbaijanis in traditional costume participating in a pre-election rally.

Marshall Cavendish Benchmark
99 White Plains Road
Tarrytown, NY 10591
Website: www.marshallcavendish.us

© Marshall Cavendish International (Asia) Private Limited 2006
® "Cultures of the World" is a registered trademark of Marshall Cavendish Corporation.

Series concept and design by Times Editions
An imprint of Marshall Cavendish International (Asia) Private Limited
A member of Times Publishing Limited

Library of Congress Cataloging-in-Publication Data
King, David C.
    Azerbaijan / by David C. King.—1st ed.
        p. cm.—(Cultures of the world)
    Summary: "An overview of the history, culture, peoples, religion, government,
        and geography of Azerbaijan"—Provided by publisher.
    Includes bibliographical references and index.
    ISBN 0-7614-2011-8
    1. Azerbaijan—Juvenile literature. I. Title. II. Series.
    DK692.3.K56 2005
    947.54—dc22   2004028443

Printed in China

7 6 5 4 3 2 1

CONTENTS

Having close familial ties is central to the Azerbaijani way of life.

3

After the war in Nagorno-Karabakh, Azerbaijani youth are looking forward to a brighter and more peaceful future.

INTRODUCTION

SOUTH OF RUSSIA, between the Caspian and Black seas, lies a mountainous region called Transcaucasia. Of the three independent republics that occupy Transcaucasia, two—Georgia and Armenia—are familiar to most Americans. But the third, Azerbaijan, seems remote and mysterious. Azerbaijan is a small country but a land of striking beauty and variety. Its many regions include the snowcapped peaks of the Greater Caucasus Mountains, fertile river valleys interlaced with irrigation canals, subtropical forests, and tea plantations in the south. In contrast, arid patches of semi-desert are found near the Caspian Sea. At times, Azerbaijan looks like a country forgotten by time. Ancient churches and mosques rise above medieval villages or the walled "old town" areas of cities. In other places, definite signs of the 21st century emerge in the glass-and-steel office buildings of modern urban centers where Internet cafés are perched on busy street corners. Azerbaijan is a nation where the ancient and the modern often exist side by side.

GEOGRAPHY

AZERBAIJAN IS A SMALL COUNTRY on the dividing line between Europe and Asia. With an area of 33,436 square miles (86,600 square km), the nation is slightly smaller than Portugal. Azerbaijan's population of 7,868,385—as estimated by the United Nations in 2004—is about the same as that of New Jersey. In terms of population density, Azerbaijan is about as crowded as California, with roughly 230 people per square mile.

The Greater Caucasus Mountains form Azerbaijan's northern border with Russia, while the Caspian Sea is the eastern boundary. To the west are Armenia and Georgia which, like Azerbaijan, are former republics of the Soviet Union. In the south, the Araks River and the Talish Mountains separate Azerbaijan from Iran.

Although the country's geography seems to be dominated by spectacular mountain ranges, more than 40 percent of Azerbaijan is lowland, or level. Although a large portion of these lowlands is arid semi-desert, irrigation makes nearly half of the total land area suitable for farming. The mild climate combined with extensive irrigation has enabled Azerbaijan to be a major food producer. Until the Soviet Union collapsed in the early 1990s, the republic accounted for about 10 percent of the entire Soviet agricultural output.

Above: **The Greater Caucasus Mountains separate Azerbaijan from Russia.**

Opposite: **Although Azerbaijan is ringed by mountains, lowlands such as this valley make up about 40 percent of the nation's landmass.**

7

A shepherd watches his flock in Dahana, one of Azerbaijan's most remote regions.

GEOGRAPHIC REGIONS

Roughly half the country is mountainous, dominated by the towering northern peaks of the Greater Caucasus Mountains. Azerbaijan's highest peaks are located there, including Bazardyuze at 14,652 feet (4,469 m). The jagged peaks and glaciers of the high mountains offer breathtaking views of the lower valleys, where rushing streams thread through spectacular gorges.

The fertile lower slopes of the mountains are covered with forests interspersed with pastureland. In the extreme northeast, however, the foothills lack the same rich, well-watered soil and give way to an arid coastal plain on the edge of the Caspian Sea.

To the south and west, the rugged Lesser Caucasus Mountains form a second important mountain system. Sparkling Lake Goygol is found in the range at the altitude of 5,138 feet (1,567 m). Bordering the peaks is the Kura River depression, a series of plains and low hills separated by the Kura and Araks rivers. This is the lowest region of Azerbaijan. In the central and eastern areas of the depression, the soil is enriched by the annual deposits of silt as the Kura empties into the Caspian Sea. The 500-mile (805-km) coastline of the Caspian has few bays or inlets. The three largest projections of land into the sea are the Abseron Peninsula, on which the capital city of Baku is situated, the Sara Peninsula, and the Kura Sandbar.

RIVERS AND LAKES

There are more than 1,000 rivers in Azerbaijan, but only about 20 are longer than 60 miles (97 km). The Kura River is by far the largest—in fact the largest in all of Transcaucasia. It flows from northwest to southeast and empties into the Caspian Sea. Most of the country's rivers are found in the depression between the Kura and Araks rivers.

The many rivers join an elaborate network of canals to irrigate large fields of cotton and grain. One major waterway is the Upper Karabakh Canal, which provides irrigation for its entire length of 109 miles (175 km), watering 250,000 acres (1,012 square km) of farmland. The canal also feeds the Mingechaur Reservoir, a mammoth lake covering 234 square miles (606 square km), with a maximum depth of more than 200 feet (61 m). The Upper Shirvan Canal, the second most important, also irrigates about 250,000 acres (1,012 square km) along its 75-mile (121-m) length.

Although there are roughly 250 lakes in Azerbaijan, all of them are small. Even the largest—Lake Haciabul, with an area of 6 square miles (15.5 square km), and Lake Boyukshor, which is 4 square miles (10.4 square km)—would disappear in the Mingechaur Reservoir.

In the south, the Araks River and the Talish Mountains form the border between Azerbaijan and Iran.

Most of the people living on the southern side of the Araks River in Iran are Azerbaijanis; in fact, they actually outnumber the population of the Republic of Azerbaijan.

THE LARGEST INLAND SEA

The sea-horse-shaped Caspian Sea (*below*) was once part of a single world ocean. It was connected to that great body of water by the Sea of Azore, the Black Sea, and the Mediterranean Sea. The rising landforms of Asia and Europe slowly and eventually isolated the saltwater Caspian in a large hollow that is more than 90 feet (28 m) below sea level.

The Caspian sprawls over an area measuring nearly 750 miles (1,208 km) from north to south, with an average width of 200 miles (322 km). Its total area—approximately 143,000 square miles (370,370 square km)—makes it slightly larger than Japan. The depth of the sea varies greatly, from 12 to 20 feet (3.7 to 6.1 m) in the north to a maximum depth of 3,360 feet (1,025 m). There is also wide variation in the water's salinity, or salt content. In the cooler north, where great Russian freshwater rivers such as the Volga and Vistula flow into the Caspian Sea, the salt content is only about 0.1 percent. In the subtropical south, where evaporation occurs at a much faster rate, the salinity level is more than 30 percent.

The ancient Romans named the sea after the Kaspi, a nomadic people who moved around its western shore. And it was the Romans who made the initial discovery of the process that turns

the eggs produced by the sturgeon into the salty delicacy known as caviar. As the sturgeon population declined in the late 20th century, all sorts of substitutes have been tried for their prized roe, but so far, nothing comes close to the real thing.

CLIMATE

Most of Azerbaijan has a subtropical climate, but there is considerable variation across the country, depending on factors such as precipitation and altitude. Summers, for example, are generally warm and dry, particularly in the central and eastern parts of the country. Along the coast of the Caspian Sea, however, rainfall amounts to only 8 to 12 inches (20.3 to 31 cm) per year, producing a semi desert climate. Farther south, in an area called the Länkärän Lowland, rainfall is between 47 and 55 inches (119.4 and 140 cm), which produces a more humid climate suitable for crops such as tea and cotton.

In other parts of the country, the climate varies a great deal with the altitude. In the extreme southeast, which is actually below sea level, the summers are long—four to five months—and very hot, with temperatures

The hot and dry climate of Azerbaijan's semi-desert areas mainly supports the growth of sparse shrubbery.

averaging 81°F (45°C) but often topping 100°F (56°C).

Farther inland, in the foothills of the mountain ranges, temperatures are milder, and annual rainfall ranges from 12 to 35 inches (30.5 to 89 cm). The higher peaks of both the Lesser and Greater Caucasus ranges are in a mountain-forest zone, where low rainfall and summer temperatures averaging 41°F (23°C) produce tundralike conditions—the kind of climate found in subarctic regions such as southern Alaska. At altitudes above 10,000 feet (3,050 m), cold temperatures and heavy snowfall keep the mountain passes closed for three or four months each year.

FLORA AND FAUNA

Variations in altitude and climate create wide differences in plant and animal life. More than 4,000 species of plants are found in Azerbaijan. The semi-desert conditions of the lowlands and the drier foothills of some mountain ranges support a variety of grasses and shrubs. Large areas of forest cover the southern slopes of the Greater Caucasus, parts of the Lesser Caucasus, and the Talish Mountains. These lush forests are home to Iberian oaks, beeches, eastern birches, albizias, and ironwoods.

Azerbaijan has a rich variety of animal life, with more than 12,000 species. In the lowlands, herds of gazelles graze the semi-desert grasses, avoiding packs of jackals and hyenas. These arid regions are also home to several species of snakes and rodents. In the Kura-Araks Valley and on the mountain slopes, roe deer and Caucasian deer are numerous, sharing their habitat with wild boars, lynx, brown bears, chamois, mountain goats (at higher elevations), and occasionally leopards.

There are also a few herds of European bison, or wisents. These shaggy creatures look much like North American bison and are actually a little larger. Like many other big-game species, wisents were overhunted—mostly in the 17th and 18th centuries—and by the mid-1900s the species was close to extinction. Most of the remaining herds are now protected in game preserves and parks.

Above: **European bison. Only about 3,000 of these animals are left in existence.**

Opposite. **Azerbaijan's thick deciduous forests are home to a diverse array of animal species.**

NAXÇIVAN: AN ISOLATED PROVINCE

Naxçivan is a small wedge of mountainous territory located between Armenia and Iran. The determination of the territory's people and the support of Baku have kept it part of Azerbaijan since the breakup of the Soviet Union in the early 1990s.

According to legend, this tiny region was founded before 1500 B.C. by Noah. It prospered under Persian rule in the Middle Ages, then was taken over by Russia in 1828, and became part of the Soviet Union. In January 1990 as the Soviet Union began to crumble, Naxçivan became the first part of the former Soviet Union to declare its independence. Within a few months, however, the people voted to become part of Azerbaijan.

The rocky mountainsides here offer breathtaking views of Iran, Armenia, and Nagorno-Karabakh. Valleys are speckled with orchards that produce apricots, pears, and peaches. But the fertile orchards and beautiful scenery are not enough for the province to overcome its isolation. Unemployment is at times as high as 50 percent, and there are long lines for emigration permits. Naxçivan's future remains highly uncertain.

The mild winters lure many flocks of birds to the shores of the Caspian Sea, and nature reserves offer a safe haven from hunters. These winter residents include flamingos, pelicans, swans, herons, egrets, sandpipers, and a variety of ducks and geese. Common inland birds are pheasant, rock partridge, and bustards.

The Caspian Sea and the Kura River support abundant fish life, but the Caspian has suffered severe environmental damage, largely from the oil-extracting practices that were in place under Soviet rule. Pollution, combined with overfishing, has greatly reduced the catch of sturgeons—fish prized for producing roe that is made into the world's best caviar. Other fish common to the Kura and the Caspian are herring, perch, and pike.

A stand of flamingos in Azerbaijan. Migratory birds are attracted to the country's mild winters.

HISTORY

AZERBAIJAN'S GEOGRAPHICAL LOCATION has had a powerful influence on its history. Situated between the Caspian and Black seas, Azerbaijan is at a vital crossroads between Asia and Europe. Great empires have collided there; and some of history's most famous conquerors have fought for the land, including Cyrus the Great, Pompey, Alexander the Great, Tamerlane, and Genghis Khan.

Rarely has Azerbaijan had the peace and stability needed to build a strong independent state. Instead, through most of its history, it has been a province ruled by Persia, Russia, or some other powerful empire.

Opposite: **A 16th-century painting depicts the nomadic lifestyle of the Turkish ancestors of the Azerbaijanis.**

Below: **A 16th-century map of the Russian empire in Asia. For centuries control of the region that would become Azerbaijan shuffled between the Persian and Russian empires.**

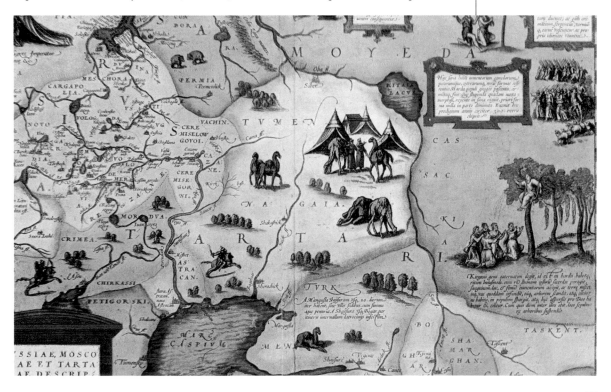

17

EARLY HISTORY

The first human settlements in what is now Azerbaijan date back to the Stone Age, more than 12,000 years ago. Hundreds of cave dwellings have been excavated throughout the country. The most impressive evidence of Stone Age life consists of more than 6,000 engravings, called petroglyphs, found on cave walls near the coast of the Caspian Sea.

CONQUEST AND CHANGE

During the fourth century A.D., missionaries from Armenia spread Christianity into the kingdom of Albania, and a large portion of the population was

The cave petroglyphs of Qobustan depict what life was like for their creators 12,000 years ago.

converted. Over the next 300 or 400 years, dozens of Christian churches were built. Ruins of these ancient structures still dot the landscape.

Christianity did not become permanent, however. In A.D. 642 Arab Muslim armies swept into Caucasian Albania. The land became part of the vast Islamic empire, which sprawled from Asia through the Middle East and into North Africa. Islam soon dominated Albania, which became a province within the empire.

In the 11th century, another Islamic power gained control. These new invaders were Turkish tribes that were part of the Seljuk dynasty. The conquest led to a blending of peoples, cultures, and languages. The original population, largely descended from Persians, began to merge with the Turks, and the Persian language was replaced by a Turkic dialect that slowly evolved into modern Azeri.

Holy Communion at an Armenian church in Nagorno-Karabakh. The ceremony has remained largely unchanged from the time Armenian missionaries began to spread the Christian faith over 1,700 years ago.

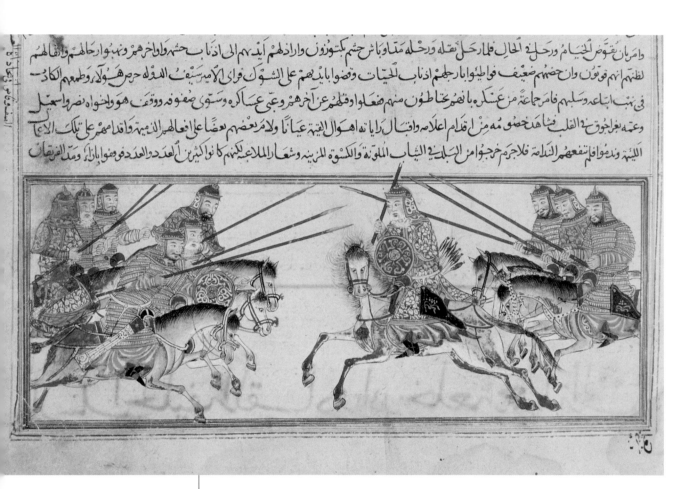

واومان يقوص الخيام ورحله المال فلما حل نقله ورحله متاواو بأرحيم لكتبونون واراذهم ايذهم الى ذنا بحشه والاخرهم هنه بواو رحالهم وقفالهم لظنهم قوفون وان حصهم ضعيف فاطيواو بارحلهم اذناب الحيات وضوا بايدهم على الشوك فواى الاميرسيف المثه حربهولى وطعمه الكاذ في نهب اتباعه وسلبهم فامم جماعة من عنكر بانصرك باطون منهم ضعلواوقلهم عن آخرهم وعتى عساكر وسوى ضعوه ووقفه وهو واخواه نصر وسعبل وعمه يغراجوق القلب فشاهذخصو مه من اقدام اعلاصه وانبال داراى ذه اهوال العنبه عبانا ولاامر بعصهم بعضا على ذعالهماالذيهم وقادمهم على تلك الاعه الليبه وندمواقلم تنفعهم النذامه فلاجرم خرجوا من العساء في الثياب الملونة والكسوة المزينه وشعار الملاعبه لكنهم كانواكثيرين العدد والعده وفهموا بازلاى ومذالفريقان

In 1236 the Mongol warriors of Genghis Khan's powerful empire conquered what is today called Azerbaijan and remained in control until 1498. Around 1500 a new Persian kingdom was formed under the Safavid dynasty, which had its capital at Tabrïz. The new rulers established the Shia (or Shiite) branch of Islam as the official religion, and this dominance continues today.

During the reign of the Safavids, Azerbaijan was frequently a battleground in a power struggle between Persia and Russia. Safavid rule ended in 1722, and northern Azerbaijan splintered into several principalities, or khanates (areas governed by a khan, or ruler). These divisions made it easier for Russia to move in and seize power. The Persians fought back in two Russo-Persian wars: in 1804–13 and 1826–28.

Above: **A page taken from a 13th-century manuscript depicts two warring Mongol tribes. Mongol warriors like these fought for a Mongol empire that stretched from East Asia to eastern Europe in the 13th century.**

Opposite: **One of the first oil wells dug in Azerbaijan. The nation's vast reserves of oil and gas have made it a country of strategic importance on the world stage.**

Russia's victories gave it control over most of northern Azerbaijan, and the Araks River became the region's permanent dividing line. This advance made Russia the first European nation to move into the Middle East. About half of the Azerbaijani people remained south of the Araks within Persia.

Under Russian rule, northern Azerbaijan began a period of development far different from what happened on the Persian side of the Araks River. When oil was discovered in the area around Baku, the modern industrial age arrived in the nation almost overnight. Baku became the center of a fantastic oil boom. Workers and oil companies swarmed into the area, creating a multiethnic boomtown in which Azerbaijanis made up less than half the population. By 1900 Azerbaijan was producing half the world's oil, and the oil-refining industry had its beginnings there. But the great boom did not last. As new sources of oil were found in other parts of Russia and the world, less and less development money was spent in Azerbaijan. Since no manufacturing industries had been set up, hundreds of workers joined the ranks of the unemployed, and the mansions of the oil barons were abandoned.

THE MYSTERY OF THE REED BOATS

Many of the Azerbaijan petroglyphs portray the daily life of the people inhabiting the shore of the Caspian Sea several thousand years ago. Some of the cave art shows reed boats, a fact that lured the famous Norwegian ethnologist Thor Heyerdahl (*above, on the right, with a reconstructed reed boat*) to the caves in 1989 and again in 1994. Heyerdahl had gained fame previously for his theories connecting ancient reed boats found in Egypt, Peru, and Polynesia.

In Azerbaijan Heyerdahl was thrilled to find that the boats depicted in caves near Qobustan were strikingly similar to reed-boat petroglyphs found in Norway. On the basis of these discoveries and other information, Heyerdahl theorized that the people of Scandinavia came originally from the coast of the Caspian Sea. While the theory is intriguing, it is not widely accepted, and many scientists are waiting until more supporting evidence is found.

Over the centuries, the forces of history have divided Azerbaijan into northern and southern halves. The roots of this division go back to the fourth century B.C. when two kingdoms were formed: Caucasian Albania (which had no connection to the Balkan state of Albania in Europe) in the north and the kingdom of Atropatene in the south. By about A.D. 200, Caucasian Albania's boundaries matched those of the modern republic of Azerbaijan. It had become a powerful kingdom with several thriving cities. Atropatene, the southern part of Azerbaijan, became part of the Persian empire and today remains within the boundaries of modern Iran.

SOVIET RULE

In 1917 a revolution brought the Russian empire to an end, and a year later the provisional democratic government was overthrown by the Bolshevik wing of the communist party. Russia became the Soviet Union. In Azerbaijan a small group of professionals, known as the intelligentsia, joined with workers in Baku to form a democratic government. But in April 1920, the Soviet Union's Red Army invaded and quickly ended Azerbaijan's brief period as an independent state.

For a few years starting in 1922, the three regions of Transcaucasia— Azerbaijan, Armenia, and Georgia—were joined in a loose federation called the Transcaucasian Soviet Federated Socialist Republic (TSFSR).

The Baku Congress of 1920 was held in Azerbaijan's capital soon after the Soviet Union took over the country. The congress advocated the spread of Communism in central Asia.

This attempt to create regional unity did not bring an end to the seething ethnic conflict that gripped a small mountainous area on the Azerbaijan-Armenia border called Nagorno-Karabakh. The conflict, which pitted Armenian Christians against Muslim Azerbaijanis, grew bitter and sometimes violent during various periods in the 20th century.

Under Soviet rule, the Azerbaijani members of the intelligentsia were given special treatment when it came to filling government jobs. With the support of Soviet communists, Azeri leaders tried to create a secular state—a society in which organized religion would have no influence. By the late 1920s, this policy became known as intolerant atheism. The Azeri government closed mosques, outlawed religious education, and imprisoned dozens of Muslim clerics.

This vicious campaign practically destroyed the institution of Islam in Azerbaijan, but the religion remained central to people's lives. The majority of Azerbaijanis continued to live according to the traditions, beliefs, and prohibitions of Islam.

In the 1930s Azerbaijan experienced a new wave of violence as Josef Stalin, dictator of the Soviet Union, began a systematic campaign to destroy all opposition to his rule. He found a

useful henchman in Mir Jafar Baghirov, first secretary of the communist party of Azerbaijan. First the intelligentsia was purged of potential enemies, then the communist party itself was. More than 100,000 Azeris were executed or sent to concentration camps in the Soviet Union. In 1936 the attempt to create a unified Transcaucasian republic ended. The Azerbaijani Soviet Socialist Republic became a separate republic within the Soviet Union.

WORLD WAR II AND AFTER

During World War II (1939–45), Germany was eager to reach the oil fields of the Soviet Union and the Middle East. In June 1941 German armies invaded the Soviet Union and reached the Greater Caucasus Mountains a year later. The Soviet Red Army, aided by Azeri and Armenian troops, managed to keep the Germans from crossing into Azerbaijan.

Another wartime event led to the possibility that Iranian Azerbaijan might be united with the Republic of Azerbaijan. In mid-1941 Soviet forces

Above: **Nazi soldiers advance towards the Caucasus during World War II. Rich oil resources made territories such as Azerbaijan targets for foreign powers.**

Opposite: **A Soviet soldier maintaining the peace at Naxçivan's border with Armenia in 1990. Prior to the collapse of the Soviet Union, tensions between Azeris and Armenians were kept in check by the Soviet army.**

Opposite: **A soldier caught in the war between the Azerbaijanis and the Armenians for Nagorno-Karabakh.**

occupied Iranian Azerbaijan, which led to a revival of unification ideas, known as the Pan-Azerbaijani movement. Soviet leaders even supported an independent Azerbaijani people's government at Tabrïz. When the war ended, however, the Western Allies, led by the United States and Great Britain, insisted that the Russians withdraw.

The brutality of Stalin's rule ended with Stalin's death and the leadership of Nikita Khrushchev (1953–64). During what was called the Khrushchev Thaw, Soviet rule of Azerbaijan became more relaxed. Censorship of the press was eased, as was control of scholarship and literature.

Although the post-Stalin era meant a lessening of dictatorial controls, Azerbaijan suffered a period of economic stagnation beginning in the 1960s. The Soviet government failed to invest any money in the declining Baku oil fields. Outdated equipment and a lack of environmental concern were transforming the western Caspian Sea into an environmental nightmare.

During the same period, the Soviets decided to make the city of Sumqayit the capital of a new petrochemical industry. The country's third-largest city produced its own ecological horror as chemicals poisoned the air, water, and land.

ETHNIC CONFLICT

In the late 1980s the seemingly indestructible Soviet Union begun to crumble. One after another, the former communist satellite states of central and eastern Europe claimed their independence. As with the rest of the Soviet republics, Azerbaijan declared its independence on August 30, 1991. The last of the Azerbaijani communist party leaders, Ayaz N. Mutalibov, was elected president of the new republic.

Hopes for a new age of independence were overshadowed, however, by the Azeri-Armenian conflict playing out along the border between the two republics. Soviet power had kept the dispute in check, but after the collapse of the Soviet Union, warfare erupted in Nagorno-Karabakh. Armenian troops, most of them trained in the Soviet army, quickly gained the upper hand. President Mutalibov was reluctant to increase the Azeri army's presence in the region for fear that he would not be able to control his forces. In 1992, when

THE WAR FOR NAGORNO-KARABAKH

Nagorno-Karabakh is a tiny patch of land within the borders of Azerbaijan. It is a place of rugged beauty: heavily forested mountains, steep-sided valleys, and picturesque farms and pastures. In 1989 the largely Armenian population voted for independence from Azerbaijan. For the next five years, Nagorno-Karabakh was the scene of bitter warfare as the outnumbered Karabakhists tried to withstand constant bombardment by Azeri and Russian forces. When the Soviet Union collapsed, the war changed dramatically. Armenian troops aided the Kharabakhist commandos and forced the Azerbaijani army to retreat.

An estimated 500,000 Azerbaijani Muslims were forced to flee. Since the cease-fire was established in 1994, Nagorno-Karabakh has struggled to rebuild, but the task seems overwhelming. Roughly 30,000 citizens were killed in the war and, in addition to widespread damage, the country is laced with hundreds of thousands of land mines. International organizations have tried to negotiate a permanent settlement, and the United States sponsored talks in Key West, Florida, in 2001. So far, no solution has been found that satisfies both Azerbaijan and Armenia.

Armenian troops massacred Azeri civilians at Xocali, Mutalibov was removed. A new president, Abulfaz Elchibey, replaced him in June 1992.

Elchibey also failed to stop the bloodshed in Nagorno-Karabakh. By early 1993 Armenia had control of nearly 20 percent of Azerbaijan's territory. The Azerbaijani military rebelled in June 1993, forcing Elchibey to flee. The former president hid in his hometown and refused to resign.

The rebellion provided the opportunity for Heydar Aliyev, chairman of the parliament, to seize power. Aliyev, a former member of the Soviet KGB had been unable to run in the presidential election because he was older than the age limit of 65. From his headquarters in Naxçivan, he built a loyal following and, while Elchibey was in hiding, went to Baku where he declared himself interim president. An election was held in October 1993, and Aliyev won an overwhelming victory.

With his power secure, Aliyev signed a cease-fire with Armenia and Nagorno-Karabakh in 1994. The arrangement left 13 percent of Azerbaijani land under Armenian control, and 800,000 Azeris became refugees in what had been their own country. Later in 1994 Aliyev concluded what was called the contract of the century—an oil contract worth $7.4 billion from a consortium of several oil companies to develop the Caspian Sea oil and gas reserves and share the proceeds with the state oil company.

Towards the end of his life, the ailing Aliyev pushed to have his son succeed him in office. Heydar Aliyev died in December 2003, and his son Ilham became president in spite of protests.

Above: **Heydar Aliyev *(center)* was a former member of the communist leadership before the country's independence.**

Opposite: **A city in the war-stricken region of Nagorno-Karabakh.**

29

GOVERNMENT

WORLD WAR I (1914–18) led to a dramatic reshaping of the maps of Europe and the Middle East. The old empires—the Russian, German, Austro-Hungarian, and Ottoman—were swept away in the violence of that conflict. Throughout those former realms, national groups rushed to declare their independence. In Transcaucasia, the Azerbaijanis issued their declaration on May 28, 1918—a date still celebrated as Independence Day (Georgia and Armenia also declared independence then).

The people of Azerbaijan, led by the intelligentsia, established a democratic government. In 1919 when the victorious Allies met at the Paris Peace Conference, they recognized this new government. U.S. president Woodrow Wilson was impressed. "There came in," he wrote, "a very distinguished group of gentlemen from Azerbaijan. I was talking to men who talked the same language that I did in respect of ideals, in respect of conceptions of liberty, in conceptions of right and justice."

This brave Azerbaijani experiment in self-government lasted only two years. In Russia the Communist Revolution established the Soviet Union in 1917; and in 1920 the Soviet Red Army invaded Transcaucasia, including Azerbaijan. By 1922 Azerbaijan was combined with Armenia and Georgia in the Transcaucasian Soviet Federated Socialist Republic. For the next 70 years, Azerbaijan was controlled by the Soviet dictatorship. The Azerbaijani people remain fiercely proud of their brief democracy. Now, in the 21st century, they hope they can re-create it.

Above: **President Woodrow Wilson at the Paris Peace Conference of 1919.**

Opposite: **A tapestry bearing the likeness of the late president Heydar Aliyev is displayed for sale. The Aliyev family still dominates politics in Azerbaijan.**

A man chips away at one of the last vestiges of Soviet rule in Azerbaijan. Soon after independence was declared many of the statues and portraits of communist heroes were removed from the towns and cities.

SOVIET RULE

From 1922 to 1991, Azerbaijan was one of the 15 republics that made up the Soviet Union. A new constitution for the republic, approved in 1937, declared that Azerbaijan was a sovereign state and equal to all other Soviet republics. In reality, however, the government of Azerbaijan had no control over foreign affairs, military matters, or long-range economic planning. There was even little self-government in terms of domestic politics, and all questions involving ideology and culture were decided in Moscow.

Even Azerbaijan's government structure was copied from that of the Soviet Union. A supreme soviet was the legislature, with members chosen from a slate of candidates approved by the communist party. The highest executive and administrative body was the council of ministers. The judiciary consisted of a supreme court and a lower court.

Like all the Soviet republics, Azerbaijan's role was to advance the welfare of the entire Soviet Union. Agriculture was promoted, for example, so that planners in Moscow could direct a percentage of all agricultural products to the parts of the USSR where they were most needed. Similarly, large sums were invested in the Baku oil fields, but when oil resources in other parts of the Soviet Union seemed more profitable, the Baku region was largely ignored, leaving a disastrous legacy of pollution.

INDEPENDENCE AND ETHNIC WARFARE

As soon as the Soviet Union began its surprising collapse, political leaders in Azerbaijan were ready. But Ayaz Mutalibov, the new republic's first president, was not prepared to deal with the deep-seated ethnic conflict between the Azeris and the Armenians.

Heydar Aliyev *(left)*, seen here with the Soviet Union's head of state Leonid Brezhnev, was a member of the secret police during communist rule.

One advantage of the years of stern Soviet rule was that it kept those ethnic and religious rivalries under control. In the spring of 1992, Mutalibov's failure to handle the problem led to his removal. The opposition Popular Front Party (PFP) assumed power and dissolved the largely communist supreme soviet, transferring authority to a 50-member national council, the upper house of the legislature.

A new president, PFP leader Abulfez Elchibey, also failed to resolve the bloody warfare in the Azerbaijani territory of Nagorno-Karabakh. Many Azeris charged his administration with corruption and incompetence. In June 1993 an anti-government uprising in the city of Ganca forced Elchibey to flee. As armed rebels advanced on Baku, the capital, the national council gave presidential powers to its new speaker, Heydar Aliyev.

From 1993 until he was succeeded by his son, President Aliyev exercised enormous power. Azerbaijanis today hope that the presidency of Ilham Aliyev, elected in October 2003, will lead to greater freedom and democracy.

THE MODERN GOVERNMENT

The structure of Azerbaijan's government, as established by its constitution, appears quite democratic, with a separation of powers among three branches: executive, legislative, and judicial. The executive branch is headed by the president, a prime minister, and the council of ministers. The legislative branch is unicameral, or consisting of only one house, with 125 members—100 elected from various districts

THE ALIYEV DYNASTY

Heydar Aliyev first rose to power in the Azerbaijani communist party, then became part of the Soviet KGB, a post in which he revealed his ruthless side during the 1960s. He became the first Azerbaijani to become a member of the politburo, the supreme body of the Soviet Union. In the spirit of greater freedom that followed the end of the Cold War, Soviet premier Mikhail Gorbachev had him removed following charges of corruption.

For a few years, Aliyev almost disappeared, but the instability that developed early in the Nagorno-Karabakh war gave him a new opportunity. He reinvented himself as a strong leader committed to developing Azerbaijan's oil wealth. From 1993 onwards, Aliyev ruled the republic with an iron hand. Opponents could not prevent him from grooming his son Ilham as his successor. Although Ilham had the reputation of being a playboy and a gambler, he became vice chairman of the state oil company, as well as the country's representative to the Council of Europe and president of the Azerbaijani Olympic committee. But the younger Aliyev is also well-educated—he has a doctorate in history—and has been very successful in business. His popularity and power could help Azerbaijan achieve prosperity, stability, and even greater democracy.

and 25 appointed from party lists. The judicial branch is headed by a supreme court, which supervises lower courts. All citizens aged 18 and over can vote, and opposition parties are represented in parliament.

In practice, the country's government is dominated by the strong presidency of the Aliyev dynasty. Heydar Aliyev was first elected president in October 1993 for a five-year term and was then reelected in 1998. The 1998 election was accompanied by charges of corruption from opposition parties. International agencies declared that the election did not meet normal standards for free and fair practices.

The criticisms of the Aliyev regime continued during his second five-year term. His government was frequently accused of intimidating voters, promoting violence against opposition leaders, and excessively controlling the media. Despite such strong-arm methods, Heydar Aliyev remained popular. He had arranged the cease-fire in 1994 that ended the violence in Nagorno-Karabakh. He had also brokered the lucrative deal with Western oil companies, and he had the economy moving in healthy directions.

In the spring of 2003, while delivering a televised speech, President Aliyev collapsed from a heart attack. He had wanted to run for reelection in October 2003, but his declining health led him to withdraw. Instead, he had his son Ilham appointed prime minister. Ilham then won a landslide victory to claim the presidency in October. The elder Aliyev died in a U.S. hospital in December 2003, as the people of Azerbaijan witnessed their new president emerge from his father's shadow.

The president of Azerbaijan, Ilham Aliyev, took the reins of power soon after his father's demise.

ECONOMY

THE ECONOMY OF AZERBAIJAN is still in a state of transition more than a decade after the country declared its independence from the Soviet Union. The transfer of ownership of land and businesses from the state to individuals has been slow and is not yet complete. By 2004 most agricultural land was in private hands. The same was true of small and medium-sized businesses. But the government continues to play a major role in the economy, especially in the control of major enterprises such as the oil industry and other energy sources.

During the years of Soviet control, there was serious mismanagement of Azerbaijan's resources. Planners in Moscow did not hesitate to use outdated equipment and methods in the rush to exploit the Baku oil fields. The result is a legacy of environmental pollution that will take years to repair. Soviet planners followed much the same methods in establishing a major petrochemical industry at Sumqayit, Azerbaijan's third-largest city, also located on the Abseron Peninsula. Yet another ecological disaster ensued.

In spite of the immense challenges, Azerbaijan's economy is strong and has great potential for future growth. Oil and natural gas reserves are huge, and Western companies will use less damaging methods and equipment to extract them. The country also has well-diversified agricultural and industrial sectors. Since 1995 the International Monetary Fund (IMF) has helped the Azerbaijani government to reduce inflation to a modest 2.5 percent in 2002 (after reaching a disastrous 1,800 percent in 1994). Also, in 2002 the republic's gross domestic product (GDP) grew at the rate of 9.8 percent, the seventh straight annual increase. The national currency, the manat, is stable against the dollar, and the budget deficit is only 0.4 percent of the GDP.

Opposite: **An oil platform in the Caspian Sea off Azerbaijan. The country's economy is dependent on oil exports, which account for about 90 percent of its export earnings.**

OIL AND OTHER NATURAL RESOURCES

Petroleum became one of the world's most important energy resources in the late 1800s, and Azerbaijan was one of the pioneers in its development. The underground oil reserves around Baku on the Abseron Peninsula were so close to the surface in some places that they bubbled up on their own. Search teams quickly found that there was even more oil—and natural gas—beneath the Caspian Sea. Foreign companies and workers rushed to join the Azerbaijani efforts and, by 1900, the Baku fields were producing roughly half the world's oil. The technology for refining the oil was also first developed in Baku. The city is still home to the many mansions built during the great oil boom.

After 1920, under Soviet rule, Azerbaijan's oil production gradually declined, although it still remained important in the late 1900s. After Azerbaijan declared its independence from the crumbling Soviet empire in 1991, the new republic's oil production suffered for several years, partly because of the antiquated Soviet equipment and also because of the ethnic conflicts between Christian Armenians and Muslim Azeris.

The deal that President Aliyev arranged in 1994–95 gives Azerbaijan an outstanding opportunity to regain its position as one of the world's leading oil producers. More than 20 companies, led by U.S. and British firms, are now part of a multi billion-dollar consortium tapping the rich deepwater oil fields that were beyond the reach of the Soviet Union's primitive equipment. They are also building a $3 billion pipeline from Baku through the republic of Georgia to the Turkish port of Ceyhan. From there, ocean tankers will take the oil to refineries in the United States, and the Azerbaijani economy will once again reap the rewards of its great oil potential.

Azerbaijan also has rich supplies of other natural resources, including natural gas, lead, zinc, iron, and copper ores, as well as building materials such as limestone and marble.

Workers attach a segment of the oil pipeline that will stretch from Azerbaijan to Turkey.

ORIGINS OF THE NOBEL PRIZE

One of the early investors in the Baku oil fields in the 1890s was Alfred Nobel, the Swedish-born inventor of dynamite and other explosives. Nobel used the fortune he acquired from these investments to establish the Nobel Prizes—the world's highest honors given in specific areas of the social and natural sciences as well as for literature and the promotion of peace.

AGRICULTURE

In spite of its small size and many mountainous regions, Azerbaijan enjoys a profitable and highly diversified agriculture. Plentiful water for irrigation and different climatic zones combine to make a wide variety of crops possible, from those that thrive in cold winters and mild summers to crops such as tea and citrus fruit that need subtropical conditions. An estimated 40 percent of the nation's landmass is suitable for agriculture, and more than half of that potential farmland is currently under cultivation.

Grain is the republic's leading crop, with raw cotton running a close second. Grapes have become increasingly important as well. Most of

Farm-workers gather hay in the Sheki region of Azerbaijan.

that crop is used to make wine—one of Azerbaijan's major exports. Other crops include spring vegetables, fruit, walnuts, and hazelnuts. Tea and citrus fruits are grown in the south, and areas around the towns of Sheki, Zagatala, and Göyçay have long been involved in the breeding of silkworms.

Under Soviet rule, Azerbaijan became one of the region's leading agricultural producers, supplying 10 percent of the total Soviet output. Since Azerbaijan's independence, farm families have turned in new directions and now raise cattle and pigs for export.

FISHERIES

Herring, pike, and perch are fished from the Kura and other rivers, and trout is found in mountain streams. But it is the Caspian Sea that is the source of one of Azerbaijan's most treasured products.

That body of water has long been world famous as a major source of caviar, which is still a valuable export. The roe is salted in order to bring out the flavor, as well as to preserve it. Beluga caviar, which comes from a particular species of sturgeon, is considered a great delicacy and ranks as one of the world's most expensive foods.

Over the past century, sturgeon fishing has declined steadily, in part because of the Caspian Sea's pollution from oil, sewage, and chemicals. Overfishing is also a major reason for the decline.

A worker packing mounds of caviar into a can. Beluga caviar, the most prized kind, is made from the roe of the beluga sturgeon, an endangered variety of fish found only in the Caspian and Black Seas.

A factory near Baku. Many factories producing equipment related to the petroleum industry have emerged in Azerbaijan since the country declared its independence.

INDUSTRY

Like Azerbaijan's agriculture, its industry is characterized by its great variety. Processing plants, for example, produce chemical fertilizers, herbicides, synthetic rubber, and plastics, as well as gasoline and kerosene. Since the 1990s, other manufacturing facilities have begun making equipment for the oil and natural-gas industry, as well as electrical equipment and all kinds of appliances. The food industry accounts for about one-third of the republic's total industrial output. A large percentage of that is wine production.

Light industries—located in Xankändi, Gäncä, and Baku—produce cotton and woolen textiles, knitwear, footwear, and a variety of consumer goods, including toys and bicycles. Handmade carpets, rugs, and leather goods have been vital components of village economies for centuries.

TRADE AND TRANSPORTATION

Azerbaijan is steadily increasing its exports of oil and natural gas, and its export rate is expected to rise even farther after the oil pipeline to the Mediterranean is completed. Other exports include chemicals, machinery, food, cotton, and some iron and steel. Imports include some food items such as milk and meat, as well as motor vehicles and machinery.

Azerbaijan has a large number of trade partners, including Russia and several of the former Soviet republics (Ukraine, Belarus, Georgia, and the central Asian countries). Other trade partners are Iran, Turkey, and, increasingly, Great Britain and the United States.

Since there are few navigable rivers in Azerbaijan, most freight is carried by railroad and truck. The Abseron region, including the peninsula and cities such as Baku and Sumqayit, is the most urbanized and industrialized part of Azerbaijan. Several highways link this region to all parts of the republic as well as to neighboring countries such as Iran, Turkey, Georgia, and Russia. Railways, with much of its mileage electrified, also carry freight from the peninsula throughout the country.

Baku is also a major port on the Caspian Sea. Bulk freight items such as grain, timber, and oil are shipped to central Asia, Russia, and Iran. There are also ferry services and passenger lines. In addition, Baku has air service to many cities in Europe and Asia.

The harbor of Baku.

ENVIRONMENT

VISITORS WHO TRAVEL by taxi or bus from the airport to Baku pass through what looks like an industrial wasteland. On one side, the travelers see the sparkling blue of the Caspian Sea, although the view is marred by offshore oil platforms and derricks. On the other side, the view is of pools of oil and sludge oozing over barren areas of land where nothing can grow. Oil slicks also mar the beaches, and even where the water looks inviting, the stench of oil reveals pollution.

These images of the Abseron Peninsula represent Azerbaijan's legacy from 70 years of Soviet rule. Throughout the 20th century, Soviet planners were intent on taking as much of the republic's oil—and other natural resources—as quickly and as cheaply as possible. The damage caused by the Soviet Union's reckless exploitation of the republic's oil resources made the Abseron Peninsula and the surrounding shoreline of the Caspian Sea one of the most polluted areas in the world.

The devastating effects of Soviet-style industry has not been confined to the natural environment. Sumqayit, an industrial town, is a tragic example of the human cost of unfettered industrial development. Residents there are more likely to develop cancer and stillbirths are commonplace.

After the Soviet Union collapsed, the new republic of Azerbaijan was left to clean up the wreckage. The task was delayed by the war in Nagorno-Karabakh, by the political upheaval that followed, and by lack of funds. While the international consortium of Western oil companies develop the oil fields and the pipeline, the Azerbaijani people hope that they can help restore the region's environment and use technology that will protect against future disasters. However, experts estimate that decontamination and rebuilding plants will cost at least $15 billion—more than half of Azerbaijan's total annual GDP. Restoring the republic's environment is expected to continue for 30 years or more.

Opposite: **A petrochemical plant discharges its waste into a canal. Although the oil industry is vital to Azerbaijan's economy, it has been harmful to the country's environment.**

45

THE SOVIET LEGACY

From about 1890 to 1915, Baku was the oil capital of the world. Then its dominance began to slide. Under Soviet rule after 1922, the Baku region experienced a steady decline. The oil still flowed, but Soviet leaders became more interested in developing other oil fields. In 1935 there was an interest in developing offshore drilling near Baku. Primitive drilling platforms were built in the Caspian, using antiquated equipment and techniques. The new burst of activity led to more accidents and increased damage to the sea and land.

A unique artifact from the days of Soviet oil plundering is the world's first offshore oil rig. Built in 1947 on massive stilts and rocks, the rig—called Neft Daşlari—was like a small city, with apartments for 5,000 workers, as well as a bakery, a school, and a movie theater. The rig still produces

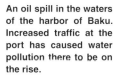

An oil spill in the waters of the harbor of Baku. Increased traffic at the port has caused water pollution there to be on the rise.

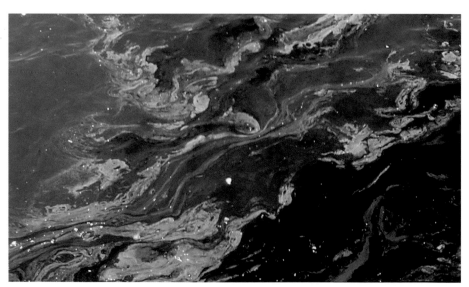

some 15,000 barrels of oil per day, about 10 percent of its earlier output.

In the 1950s, as oil production declined again, Soviet planners shifted their focus to a new part of the republic. A large portion of the Soviet Union's petrochemical industry was moved to Sumqayit. At its peak, Sumqayit was a booming industrial town, creating a new wave of prosperity but at an enormous cost. Scores of factory chimneys spewed ugly brown and yellow clouds, producing a permanent unhealthy haze. In addition to oil slicks and polluted air and water, there were growing reports of people, especially children, contracting fatal diseases and an alarming increase in birth defects.

With independence and the end of Soviet control, most of the factories were shut down. This led to high unemployment and economic hardship for the people of Sumqayit. But cleanup efforts are under way, and the air and water have improved. Several newly formed environmental organizations have spearheaded the restoration efforts, although they are hampered by lack of funds.

The greatest hope for re-creating a healthy environment in the Abseron region may be the steadily increasing amounts of foreign investment. More than 20 Western companies are involved in the Baku oil fields. Both Baku and Sumqayit are growing again, and residents are confident that new equipment and techniques and greater awareness of environmental impact will prevent the kind of damage the region experienced in the past. Although the air is already cleaner, more time is needed to restore beaches and devastated land areas.

A sign at one of the last operational chlorine plants in Sumqayit warns visitors of the toxic substances produced inside.

RESTORING FARMLAND

Another environmental problem Azerbaijan inherited from Soviet rule is serious land pollution. In the effort to increase agricultural production on government-controlled farmland, toxic defoliants were used to clear forests for crops, and DDT was used long after it had been discontinued in other countries. These toxic substances not only poisoned the soil but also leached into the groundwater, polluting streams, ponds, and lakes.

Safer farming methods are now in place, and several pesticides and herbicides have been banned. So far, however, few funds have been allocated for major cleanup and prevention programs. A number of international agencies have begun to provide some assistance.

Rural Azerbaijanis harvesting wheat. State-run Soviet farms, rather than small-scale farms, inflicted most of the environmental damage in Azerbaijan.

WILDLIFE PROTECTION

In the years since declaring independence, the Azerbaijani people have become increasingly committed to restoring the environment and protecting wildlife. There are now 14 nature reserves, four national parks, and 20 restricted natural habitats.

The protected natural habitats are of special interest because they help to safeguard some of the species that are endangered or threatened, like the leopard and the wisent. Similarly, the Shirvan National Park, established in 2003 as the latest addition to the system, preserves the only natural habitat for the wild Caucasian antelope.

Azerbaijanis have traditionally been hunters, and there are several popular big-game species, including bears, wild boars, and several kinds of deer. In addition, oil-field workers and telecommunications specialists

Besides setting up nature reserves and parks, the Azerbaijani government has also launched an ambitious reforestation campaign.

49

from Russia and several other countries find the nature reserves ideal places for hunting, particularly since reserves in many countries are off-limits to hunters. The most popular trophy among foreign hunters seems to be the eastern Caucasian ibex, or *tur*.

Both overhunting and overfishing have created trouble in the past, but in the 21st century poaching has become a more serious problem. This is especially true when it comes to the illegal harvesting of Caspian Sea sturgeons. The Convention on International Trade in Endangered Species has listed all varieties of sturgeon as endangered, and the fines for poaching are stiff.

A poached bear cub caged in Baku.

CASPIAN SEA STURGEON

There are a number of subspecies of sturgeon located throughout the Northern Hemisphere, including several in the Caspian Sea. They range greatly in size, with many species less than 24 inches (61 cm) long and others more than 10 feet (3 m) long and weighing 500 pounds (227 kg).

Three or four subspecies of Caspian sturgeon, especially beluga, are prized for their black or gray roe, which is used for caviar. Adding just the right amount of salt and finding the exact temperature for storing the roe without freezing it are essential for preparing the delicacy. There have been many caviar imitations: the red roe of salmon is sold as "red caviar," and often the roe of whitefish has been dyed black with the ink of cuttlefish, but true caviar experts are never fooled.

AZERBAIJANIS

AZERBAIJAN'S LOCATION at one of the major crossroads between Asia and Europe has led to a remarkable blending of peoples, religions, and languages. This mixing has been continuous since prehistoric times, and it is reflected in the makeup of the nation today, which includes members of more than 70 ethnic groups.

By far the largest group is the Azeris, who constitute more than 80 percent of the country's 7,868,385 people, according to a 2004 United Nations estimate. Other major groups, with rough estimates of their share of the population, include Dagestanis (3.2 percent), Russians (2.5 percent), Armenians (2 percent), and Lezghians (2 percent). Other groups, many of which represent only a few thousand people, include Avars, Ukrainians, Tatars, Talysh, Georgians, and Kurds.

But both the size and ethnic makeup of the nation's population have been changing over the past decade. The upheaval that accompanied independence and the warfare over Nagorno-Karabakh have led to dramatic shifts in population. After independence, for example, many Russians and other Slavic people moved back to Russia or to other former Soviet republics. This led to a 50 percent reduction in the Russian population of Azerbaijan.

The 1992–94 war over Nagorno-Karabakh pitted Azeri Muslims against Armenian Christians. Thousands of Armenians left Azerbaijan for Armenia, both during and after the conflict. In addition, when the Azerbaijani military effort collapsed in 1994, an estimated 800,000 Azeris left the war torn province.

Because of these fluid conditions, it is hard to measure the country's population growth rate. The Azeris traditionally have had a high birthrate, but in recent years this probably has been largely offset by the unusually high rate of emigration.

Opposite: **A rural Azerbaijani woman. About half of Azerbaijan's population lives in the countryside.**

Three Azeri men donning traditional hats called *papakhas*.

THE AZERI MAJORITY

Azerbaijan is the least densely populated of the Transcaucasian states, and nearly half the population is spread over rural areas. The most densely populated region is the Abseron Peninsula, where the major cities are located. Greater Baku is the largest, with about 2 million people. Gäncä is the second largest, with about 300,000, and Sumqayit has about 270,000.

In the sixth century A.D., large bands of nomads traveling by camel and horse swept across the arid steppes of south-central Asia. The Chinese called these people T'uchüeh, which has been translated as Turkish. The Turkish bands built a strong empire that stretched from Mongolia and northern China westward to the Black Sea.

One large Turkish group settled on the western shore of the Caspian Sea, where they mixed with the indigenous population, a group that traced its ancestry back more than 1,000 years to ancient Persia. Over several centuries the two factions blended into today's Azeri population, with the Turkish culture and language dominant.

From about A.D. 600 to 1600, other nomadic groups pushed across the Asian deserts and steppes. Some bands were merchants, traveling in long camel caravans. (It was with such caravans that Marco Polo traveled to the empire of Genghis Khan in China, returning to Europe with tales of the wonders and riches of Asia.) Other bands, including the Huns and Khazars, came westward as conquerors. These warlike groups often uprooted established communities, as whole societies fled the "hordes." This led to more Turkish groups settling in Azerbaijan. North of the Caucasus Mountains, fleeing peoples also pressed into Europe.

One group of conquerors was the Arab Muslims who made the entire region part of the great empire of Islam in the late 600s. The Seljuk Turks took control in the 11th century. Except for about 200 years under Mongol rule, Azerbaijan continued to be dominated by Turkish government and culture.

ETHNIC ENCLAVES

Many of the country's minority groups have tended to live close together, much as immigrant groups have done after coming to America. In Azerbaijan, however, this geographic proximity has often continued for centuries. A few of these ethnic groups have also remained quite isolated from the mainstream of society. The Xinalig, for example, numbering only a few thousand, have continued to live in a cluster of villages high in the Caucasus Mountains. Their customs and language have changed very little since the Middle Ages.

A painting of the palace of the khan of Baku. Like their subjects, the ancient rulers of Azerbaijan had Turkish roots.

Unlike the Xinalig people, most members of minority groups have considerable contact with other minorities, but still tend to live in identifiable enclaves. Nearly 150,000 Lezghians (or Lezgins) live in a number of towns and villages scattered along the northeastern border with Russia and on the southern slopes of the Greater Caucasus Mountains. Many of these towns have two or more neighborhoods in which other minorities live. In addition, about 50,000 Lezghians have moved to Baku and other major cities, but most still consider "home" to be the town or village where family members continue to live.

Another large minority, the Dagestanis, also tend to live in recognizable enclaves in the north, both in the mountains and on the narrow coastal plain bordering the Caspian Sea. Their original homeland of Dagestan is located on the northern slopes of the Greater Caucasus Mountains. Many

A group of Dagestani men.

Dagestani families raise sheep on terraced hillsides, and their craftspeople combine the wool with cotton to weave world-renowned small floor coverings called Dagestan rugs.

Another large minority, the Talysh, live in southern Azerbaijan near the border with Iran. Like the Azeri population, the Talysh are divided by the Iran-Azerbaijan border, with more than 1 million Talysh living on the Iran side and perhaps half as many residing in Azerbaijan. Most Talysh live in small towns or in mountain villages, where ancient traditions and handicrafts—including the famous Talysh carpets—have been maintained for hundreds of years. Farmers in the lush semi-tropical valleys operate tea plantations and also have orchards of citrus fruit trees and *feijoas*, fruit-bearing shrubs. The Talysh people are of Persian ancestry, and they speak an Indo-European language. This sets them apart from the majority of Azerbaijanis, whose background and language are Turkic, and also from East Caucasian language groups such as the Lezghians and Dagestanis.

The mountainous Länkärän-Talish region is the traditional home of most of the ethnic Talysh in Azerbajian.

KURDS, A SPECIAL MINORITY

The traditional lands that make up Kurdistan, which has never been a nation of its own, are spread across the mountainous regions of Iran, Iraq, and Turkey, with smaller enclaves in Syria and Azerbaijan.

The Kurds are a distinct ethnic group, with their own language and unique cultural heritage. Traditionally the Kurds were sheepherders whose craftspeople were known for handwoven rugs, carpets, and saddlebags. Through the years, they have come to depend increasingly on agriculture.

The Kurdish people are renowned for their weaving skills.

The Kurds are a resilient people who, for centuries, have longed to create their own nation. Although they have occupied the area known as Kurdistan for approximately 1,500 years, they have never realized or achieved political unity. Instead of having a standing army, various tribes have earned a reputation for their military prowess. The best known Kurdish military leader, and one of the great heroes of Islam, was Saladin who lived from A.D. 1137 to 1193.

During the second Crusade, when Christian knights and soldiers tried to capture the Holy Land from the Muslims, Saladin led a brilliant counterattack in 1187. The stunned Christians lost all but a tiny foothold in the eastern Mediterranean. Against the next Crusade, led by England's king Richard "the Lionhearted," Saladin again proved his military skill by fighting a larger European army to a draw. He

Saladin was a Kurdish leader who fought and defeated the crusaders led by king Richard of England.

The late president Heydar Aliyev reading a prepared statement at the international conference aimed at brokering peace between Azerbaijan and Armenia in 2001. The president of Armenia, Robert Kocharian *(right)* also attended the talks.

also surprised his enemies with the extraordinary kindness he extended to prisoners as well as to the wounded and sick.

ETHNIC CONFLICTS

Most ethnic minorities have lived peacefully with the majority Azeris. The most serious internal conflicts have involved religion as well as ethnicity.

Until the collapse of the Soviet Union, the Soviet leadership maintained order. As soon as that authority was gone, violence erupted in Nagorno-Karabakh. In the ensuing civil war between Azeris and Armenians, more than 30,000 lives were lost.

Although a truce ended the open warfare in 1994, the basic conflict continues to seethe beneath the surface. Former U.S. secretary of state Colin Powell chaired an international conference on the problem in Florida in 2001, but after more than a year of negotiations no settlement was reached. Nagorno-Karabakh, which accounts for roughly 10 percent of Azerbaijan's land, remains under the control of an Armenian army. Sniper fire and land mines are a constant threat, claiming about 100 lives every year.

A somewhat similar situation exists in Naxçivan. In 1924 this small mountainous territory was made into an Autonomous Soviet Socialist Republic by the Soviet Union. This gave the Azeri people living there protection from the Armenian population surrounding them.

Armenian militiamen at Armenia's border with Azerbaijan's Naxçivan province. Despite being separated from Azerbaijan by Armenian territory, Naxçivan remains under Azerbaijani control.

61

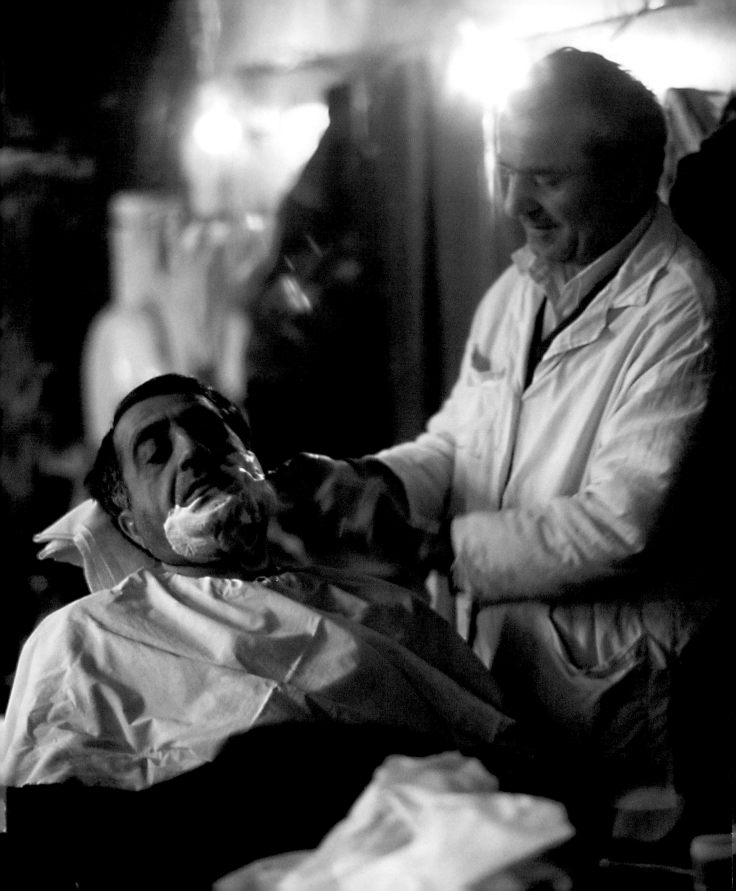

LIFESTYLE

AZERBAIJANIS TAKE GREAT PRIDE in their country. Even though Azerbaijan has been independent only since 1991, Azerbaijanis feel that their nation has existed for more than a thousand years, despite being ruled by outside powers for most of that time. Now with their own government, they express remarkable confidence in the future. There is a feeling of energy and excitement, especially in Baku and other cities, where new buildings and new businesses seem to emerge every day.

At the same time, however, there is something relaxed and casual about Azerbaijani life. People still like to take their time over a festive meal or an evening stroll. According to veteran world travelers, Azerbaijan seems like a European country in its economic growth and energy, but more like a traditional agrarian society in its laid-back lifestyle.

Above: **Fountain square in Baku. Life in the capital city is more hectic than in other Azerbaijani cities.**

Opposite: **A man gets a shave from a barber in Baku. Although the pace of development has hastened after the country's independence, the Azerbaijani lifestyle remains generally relaxed.**

Other apparent contradictions exist in the Azerbaijani character. Despite having a reputation for being hot-blooded, quick-tempered, and suspicious of strangers, foreign visitors find Azerbaijanis to be friendly and outgoing, eager to open their homes to outsiders. The true Azerbaijani character is probably a combination of these varied elements.

The Azerbaijanis' approach to Islam is also contradictory. For instance, many Azeris drink alcohol, a practice that would be forbidden in most other Muslim countries. Similarly, some Muslim women wear Western-style clothing, while others prefer more traditional Muslim dress.

The appearance of contradictions in the Azerbaijani character is probably a result of the great changes the country has witnessed. New ideas and new ways of doing things are challenging traditions and forcing people to make rapid adjustments in their attitudes and daily lives.

LIFE IN BAKU

Although Baku is still troubled by severe environmental pollution, Azerbaijan's capital is a vibrant, growing city—one of the most colorful and exciting in the former Soviet Union. Every jetliner arriving from Europe, Japan, or China brings new businesspeople, oil experts, or telecommunications specialists. New business centers and office towers are constantly emerging against a background of ancient palaces, churches, and mosques.

Not everything in the city is up-to-date. In fact, Baku's charm lies in its lively mixture of ancient and modern. In addition to constructing glistening new buildings, there is an ambitious effort to preserve the old. One major restoration project involves repairing the fantastic mansions built during the oil boom of the late 1800s.

Baku was built on natural terraces leading down to the deep turquoise of the Caspian Sea. Its physical layout offers many views of outstanding architecture dating back a thousand years. The most remarkable part of the city, for residents and visitors alike, is the magical Old Town—Icari Sahar. This is a walled neighborhood of narrow, twisting cobblestone streets where craftspeople and

merchants hawk handcrafted rugs, brassware, copper, ceramics, and antiques. Foreign visitors and Azerbaijani families can spend hours amid the stalls and shops or touring famous historic sites including the Carpet Museum, the Palace of the Shirvanshahs, and the mysterious Maiden's Tower. The entire Old Town is listed as a UNESCO world heritage site.

Outside the walls of Old Town is an area along the shore that residents call simply the *bulva*, or boulevard. This parklike setting is where Bakunian families come for evening walks. Fountain Square is a popular gathering place where there is a small fairground geared to children. The current economic boom in Baku offers plenty for kids to enjoy. Teenagers are drawn to the minicars and motorbikes for rent at Fisherman's Wharf. There are two new McDonald's and a child-oriented complex called Zoom, which includes a play area, an arcade, and a café.

Above: **The newly restored Palace of the Shirvanshahs in Baku is popular with locals and tourists alike.**

Opposite: **With increased foreign investment in Azerbaijan, a new class of affluent city-dwellers has emerged.**

OTHER CITY LIFESTYLES

Daily life in other Azeri cities is often quite different from daily life in Baku. The pace of life is slower as is the rate of economic growth. However, each of these urban centers is unique. Gäncä, for example, the country's second-largest city with a population of 300,000, is probably the place that best represents Azerbaijan's strong nationalistic spirit.

In 1804 the name of the city was changed to honor the wife of the czar, and in 1935 the Soviets renamed it Kirovabad. As soon as independence was announced in 1991, the city quickly restored the Azeri name of Gäncä. Since then, workers have carefully removed every detail of Soviet decoration on the massive Town Hall, replacing it with Azeri patriotic symbols. As in the other smaller cities, there are few job opportunities

Right: **Despite the various renamings Gäncä has undergone through the years, the heart of the city has stayed essentially the same.**

Opposite: **An abandoned factory in Sumqayit. With the dissolution of the Soviet Union, many factories in the city shut down, leaving a large portion of residents unemployed.**

in Gäncä, especially for young people. Educational facilities have not developed fast enough to equip students with 21st-century skills. The result is unemployment that has reached 50 percent, at its height. Many young people spend their time hanging out on the Ganza Küçsi, a shopping street, sharing tea, jam, and strong cigarettes.

Sumqayit is also experiencing a major economic depression, in this case because of the loss of the Soviet petrochemical industry. But that decline has been offset by a steady improvement in the quality of the air and water. The increase in foreign investment in iron and steel plants promises to stimulate the economy. However, most of the skilled and supervisory jobs are going to foreign workers who are better trained.

The city of Shemaka has faced similar difficulties. Located in beautiful hill country, dotted with picturesque vineyards, Shemaka was once the center of the Soviet wine and cognac industry. The loss of Soviet markets led to a sharp economic decline, but the people are working hard to reclaim their prosperity.

Quba, a city of approximately 22,000, includes a thriving Jewish community. The city itself, with its neat rows of old Russian

houses, seems like a quiet retirement community, with a relaxed and easygoing way of life. Many families work from their homes, making handwoven rugs. Conditions are slowly improving as the local economy gradually recovers.

RURAL LIFE

Nearly half the country's population lives in small towns and farm villages. Although there are many different kinds of farms, including grain and cotton farms, vineyards, and vegetable and livestock farms, rural life tends to follow similar patterns. People rise early and take advantage of the hours of sunlight. Their diet is simple, centering mostly on vegetables, fruit, and milk products, such as yogurt. Their normal beverage is spring water, and they drink wine in the evening. Most rural people, including children, bathe almost every day, often in cold rivers or streams. It is said to be an extremely healthy lifestyle, and Azerbaijanis are famous for their long life span.

AZERBAIJAN'S "LONG-LIFERS"

The mountain air, the varied climate, and a diet of fruit, vegetables, and milk products have enabled Azeris and Armenians to live unusually long lives. Just after World War II, Soviet sociologists and demographers began reporting that surprising numbers of people in Transcaucasia were living past 100, especially in Azerbaijan where they estimated that 44 of every 100,000 people lived past 100. In the 1950s the Soviet newspaper *Pravda* began publishing photos of *dolgozhiteli* ("long-lifers"), celebrating their 140th, 150th, or even 160th birthdays.

Some scientists, including a few Americans, were skeptical. Others believed the reports. One researcher, Dr. Alexander Leaf of Massachusetts General Hospital in Boston, was so impressed by what he saw during a visit that he wrote a book, *Youth in Old Age*, confirming the claims of longevity.

But then Dr. Leaf noticed an obituary picture of one individual, followed in succeeding years by the same photos and articles congratulating him on his 168th birthday, then his 169th and 170th. "I was gullible," Dr. Leaf admitted.

The overblown reports and claims have blurred the truth. Most researchers agree that the hardy lifestyle of mountain Azeris—and Armenians—does enable them to remain robust at least into their 80s and 90s. And it is quite likely that some individuals do live past 100 or 110. But scientists warn that the reports of "long-lifers" celebrating birthdays of 130 or beyond are not to be believed.

FAMILY LIFE

Family is central to Azerbaijani life, in cities as well as in rural areas. People of all ages spend their free time with their family, and this includes the extended family as well as the primary unit of parents and children. Going out to dinner is likely to involve 20 or more family members spending hours in a garden restaurant.

As more people move to Baku and other cities, maintaining those close ties becomes more difficult. When it is time to find a job, however, the urban newcomer is most likely to turn to members of the extended family for help. These kinship ties remain important in matters of personal advancement involving business or politics.

Familial bonds remain strong in Azerbaijan despite the rapid rate of economic progress.

EDUCATION

In the early 20th century, Azerbaijanis displayed little interest in formal education. As late as 1917, only about 10 percent of the people were literate, that is, able to read and write.

The picture changed dramatically when the Soviet Union seized control in the early 1920s. Communist authorities placed great importance on education, and an ambitious program of school construction was carried out. By 1959 elementary school was free and compulsory, and 97 percent of the people were literate. In 1966 universal secondary education was introduced, much of it in vocational schools. Russian-language schools were also introduced, in an effort to expand the role of Russian culture in Azerbaijan.

A teacher quizzes a young Azerbaijani school-boy on his math skills.

Over the past few decades, Azerbaijani higher education has become well regarded. The higher-education facilities include Rasulzade (formerly Kirov) State University, the Polytechnic Institute, the Institute of the Petroleum and Chemical Industry, the Medical Institute, and the Hajibayli Conservatory, all in Baku. In the early 1990s there were 18 higher and 77 secondary specialized-educational institutions, with a total enrollment of 168,000.

The Azerbaijani Academy of Sciences, established in 1945, directs most research activity. It is divided into a number of different sections and specialized institutions, such as the Institute of History, the Nazami Institute of Language and Literature, and the Institute of Economics. These organizations provide the latest research data to schools, medical facilities, and businesses.

RELIGION

AZERBAIJAN IS ONE of the most liberal countries with a Muslim majority. In many Muslim countries, such as neighboring Iran, religious leaders exert a powerful influence over government and society. This is not the case in Azerbaijan, which remains a secular society, controlled by civilian political leaders. In addition, even though more than 90 percent of Azerbaijanis consider themselves Muslims, many do not follow the practice of Islam closely.

The third-largest religious group is made up of the followers of different Christian churches. They form roughly 5 percent of the population. The Armenian minority, which has declined by half since the 1992–94 war in Nagorno-Karabakh, consists mostly of followers of the Armenian Apostolic Church. Other Christians belong to the Russian or the Greek Orthodox churches.

For many years, both Azeris and Armenians prided themselves on how well Muslims and Christians could get along. Nagorno-Karabakh was a mostly Armenian province surrounded by Azeri Muslim villages and towns. The collapse of Soviet control apparently allowed deep-seated conflicts to rush to the surface, resulting in the bloody civil war. One of the most urgent issues facing Azerbaijanis and Armenians is to find a way to resolve this Muslim-Christian conflict.

Above: **The ruins of the sixth-century church in Sheki. It is possibly the oldest Christian church in the Caucasus.**

Opposite: **Muslim men worship in a mosque in Azerbaijan.**

73

A group of Azerbaijani women recites the Koran in a mosque. Muslim women are required to wear a headscarf when worshiping in a mosque.

ISLAM

Islam is divided into two main branches: Shiite and Sunni. In Azerbaijan, roughly 70 percent of the people are Shiite, and a little more than 20 percent are Sunni. One difference between the two branches is that Sunni leadership depends on consensus, while Shiites believe that leaders are selected by divine right. This division causes trouble in some Muslim countries, but a spirit of tolerance prevails in Azerbaijan. In Baku, for example, the mosques serve both Shiites and Sunnis.

Islam was introduced to Azerbaijan in A.D. 642, early in the creation of the great Islamic empire, which stretched from Spain in the west across North Africa and Asia to the South Pacific. Shia (Shiite) Islam was made the official religion in the 16th century. The religion was established by the Prophet Muhammad in the early 600s A.D., and the Islamic holy book, the Koran, is considered the word of Allah (God) as revealed to Muhammad. Muslims recognize Jewish and Christian figures—including Abraham, Moses, and Jesus—as earlier prophets, but consider Muhammad the last and, by far, the most important.

The word *Islam* means "submission to the will of Allah." This submission includes acceptance of the Five Articles of Faith: belief in one God, angels, the revealed book, the prophets, and the Day of Judgment. All Muslims are to practice the Five Pillars of Islam: to recite the entire profession of faith at least once in one's lifetime, to observe the five daily calls to public prayer, to pay the *zakat* tax to benefit the poor, to fast from dawn to dusk during the holy month of Ramadan, and to make the pilgrimage (or hajj) to Mecca at least once in one's lifetime, unless prevented by health or finances.

RAMADAN

The month of Ramadan is the most holy period in the Islamic year, an observance of the time during which the Koran was revealed to Muhammad. This takes place in the ninth month of the Islamic year, which follows the lunar calendar. So the exact 30-day period during which Ramadan is observed is different each year.

Muslims show their obedience to God's will by observing a strict fast from first light in the morning until dark. Part of the day is spent in prayer, both with family members and in a mosque. As soon as it is dark, Azeri Muslims break the fast with family and friends, often with a long meal interspersed with prayer. In Baku and other cities, the festive meal can continue far into the night.

SOVIET RULE AND ISLAM

During the 70 years of Soviet rule, roughly from 1921 to 1991, communist authorities tried to crush organized religion in all parts of the Soviet empire. In Azerbaijan, the effort to suppress Islam was especially vigorous during the 1930s. Mosques were closed or destroyed, religious leaders were persecuted, and religious observances were officially condemned.

A strong Islamic revival began in the 1980s. In part, this was a way of protesting Soviet rule, but it also represented a desire to return to more basic or fundamental Islamic beliefs. In some Muslim countries, such as

The Imam Husein Mosque in the center of Baku was one of only two mosques left intact and functioning under Soviet rule. The other was Taza Pir mosque.

Iran, this religious resurgence led to the creation of an Islamic state and a rejection of modern trends such as materialism or equal rights for women. The religious revival in Azerbaijan, while not as profound or sweeping as in Iran, has continued as a more determined effort to observe Islamic practices. Mosques have been restored and new ones constructed. The five daily calls to prayer are answered by more people than in the past, and there is increased attendance at mosque services.

ANCIENT TRADITIONS

In the mountain villages of Azerbaijan, ancient beliefs and traditions are sometimes mixed with local beliefs and lore. One example of this blending can be witnessed at Beşbarmaq Daĝ ("Five-Finger Mountain"), which towers above an ancient trade route in northern Azerbaijan. The

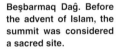
Beşbarmaq Daĝ. Before the advent of Islam, the summit was considered a sacred site.

A painting depicting the Zoroastrians of the Caucasus. Though many of the rituals that Zoroastrians practice involve fire, followers do not actually worship fire but rather a single god that is symbolized by fire.

summit of Beşbarmaq is a *pir*, or holy site. Crowds of visitors make their way up perilous rocky paths to find the holy men, in white robes and caps, each in his own rocky nook marked only by a few blankets, fluttering ribbons, and a samovar. The people come hoping to have a special wish granted, such as wanting good health, a child, or good fortune. The holy men chant prayers and dispense bits of wisdom that combine elements of Islam and ancient beliefs such as animism—the idea that there are spirits in all natural objects and events.

Similar holy places are scattered throughout Azerbaijan, especially in the mountains. Some of these include elements of Zoroastrianism, an ancient religion (sixth century B.C.) that spread from Iran and Azerbaijan to India. Zoroaster was a priest in Persia who developed an elaborate theology of monotheism or belief in one god. Jews and Christians regarded him as an astrologer, mathematician, prophet, and a major heretic. When Azerbaijan and Persia became Muslim, Zoroastrianism was tolerated for about 300 years, but then persecution led most followers to flee to India.

One of the beliefs of Zoroastrianism that has been integrated into a few small Azerbaijani sects is that Zoroaster carried sacred fires to many parts of the world. There are many places around the oil fields where jets of natural gas have created long-lasting flames. The Ateşgah Fire Temple in the village of Suraxani was built over one of these jets where, it is said, the flame has been sustained for more than 1,200 years. A handful of Zoroastrians continues to maintain the temple.

The fire at the Ateşgah Temple has never been extinguished.

THE UNUSUAL LEGACY OF ZOROASTER

Zoroaster was a priest in Persia in the sixth century B.C. Not much is known about him or his life, but he had a powerful effect on history. He lived in a time when most religions were polytheistic, that is, people believed in many different gods. Zoroaster worked out a complex philosophy and religion based, instead, on monotheism, the belief in one god. He also developed the concept of dualism in religion—the belief that the universe is controlled by two forces—Good and Evil. This belief system influenced the development of Judaism, Christianity, and Islam.

Zoroaster is also said to have been one of the originators of astrology, the practice of reading cosmic signs as a way of predicting future events, and is believed to have had a hand in developing the field of magic. He also influenced classical civilization in ancient Greece. The Greeks considered him a skilled healer, craftsman, and agriculturist, as well as an esteemed philosopher, mathematician, astrologer, and magician.

The Zoroastrian faith became the main religion of Persia (present-day Iran) until the emergence of Islam in the seventh century a.d. Muslim persecution soon forced followers of the religion to flee. The largest numbers migrated to India where, in the Mumbai (formerly Bombay) region, they developed into a well-educated wealthy community known as the Parsees. Gradually, after 1800, small groups of Zoroastrians began to move back to Iran, while some, moving farther north into Azerbaijan, found the keepers of the temple flames still at their posts in the Ateşgah Fire Temple on the Abseron Peninsula. The remnants of Zoroastrianism that exist today are just one example of the mysterious mixing of folk beliefs and ancient religions found throughout Azerbaijan.

Young Azerbaijani Jews attend religious classes.

JEWS

Jews make up a small percentage of the country's population. About half of the nation's Jews live in a few mountain towns across the Qudiyalçay River from the small city of Quba in northeastern Azerbaijan. These are the so-called Mountain Jews. They have lived in this region for many centuries. Some legends associate them with the biblical figure Noah, while others depict them as one of the lost tribes of Israel. Through isolation, their language has developed from the nation's Turkic into an Indo-European language called Judeo-Tat. The Mountain Jews have generally lived in peace with other groups, although they have been persecuted at times in the past. The other Azerbaijani Jews live in the cities, especially Baku. Many have professional or administrative positions. The Jewish population has been declining steadily since about 1990, largely in reaction to major events. The breakup of the Soviet Union led several thousand Jews to emigrate, for example, mostly from Baku to Israel. The mid-1990s warfare in Nagorno-Karabakh caused many more to leave. The number of Jews in Azerbaijan has now declined to about 30,000.

CHRISTIANS

Christians make up less than 5 percent of the country's population, and they are split among several different branches of the Eastern or Orthodox Christian Church. Most of the differences among the various churches are ancient, dating back as far as the fifth century A.D., and involve varying interpretations of the divinity of Jesus.

One of the most noticeable differences among the Christian churches involves the celebration of Christmas. While some churches follow the Roman Catholic practice of celebrating it on December 25, others, like members of the Armenian Apostolic Church, have chosen Epiphany, on January 6 (the date marking the baptism of Jesus). Two or three small churches celebrate Christmas on January 19, following the older Julian calendar.

A 19th-century Christian church in Azerbaijan. Most Azerbaijani Christians are ethnic Armenians.

LANGUAGE

MORE THAN 90 PERCENT of Azerbaijan's population speaks Azeri, which is part of a language family known as Turkic. Azeri shares much of its grammar and vocabulary with Turkic. In fact, a visitor from Turkey could travel through Azerbaijan with only a few language difficulties.

The written form of Azeri has gone through several fundamental changes. Originally, it was written in a modified form of Arabic script. In 1918, when Azerbaijan enjoyed its first brief period of independence, the Arabic was quickly replaced with a Latin alphabet similar to one being used at that time in Turkey. In 1939 the communist government of the Soviet Union ordered the use of the Cyrillic alphabet. This remained the law until 1991, when a revived Azeri Latin alphabet was restored.

Many Azerbaijanis also speak Russian, especially older people who grew up under Soviet rule, when Russian was commonly taught in the schools. Since independence, English has become increasingly popular.

In addition, there are more than 20 other languages spoken by ethnic minorities, and most of these cannot be understood by speakers of Azeri. In the Middle Ages, Arab geographers called the Caucasus Mountains *jebel al alsine*, "the mountain of languages," because there were so many different languages, dialects, and alphabets. Arabic, Latin, and Cyrillic were in use. Today, some of the less common languages and dialects, such as Talysh and Lezghian, are each spoken by more than 100,000 people. Others, such as Rutul,

Above: **Two Azerbaijani friends reading the daily news. Azerbaijanis now use a Latin script.**

Opposite: **Azerbaijanis have a range of newspapers and other publications to keep them entertained and informed.**

Tabassaran, and Dargwa, are known to only a few thousand people, who firmly insist on their right to preserve their cultures, including their languages.

HISTORICAL INFLUENCES

Many of today's languages had their origins centuries ago in the lands of eastern Asia. One family of languages, known as the Altaic languages, began east of the Altai Mountains, an imposing mountain range in central Asia. When nomadic groups moved out of Manchuria and northern China, they carried their languages and customs with them. Three major language groups, all part of the Altaic family, spread in that way: the Mongolian, the Manchu-Tungusic (in China), and the Turkic.

The groups speaking various Turkic languages moved westward, some settling in Azerbaijan, some setting down roots in other areas, including Turkey. Still other bands of nomads spread different groups of languages such as Indo-European, Caucasian, and Iranian.

The relative isolation of various groups has also influenced the development of language in Azerbaijan. Groups such as the Lezghians and Dagestanis spoke East Caucasian languages, and other groups such as the Talysh and Kurds spoke Indo-European languages. As these groups became isolated from the others, especially in mountainous regions, their languages tended to change little, unless there was significant contact with traders from other language groups.

The result of this linguistic isolation is that some of the languages spoken in Azerbaijan have almost nothing in common with one another or with Azeri. Azerbaijan's Armenian minority, for example, speaks an Indo-European language heavily influenced by Persian. Not only is the spoken Armenian impossible for Azeri speakers to understand, but the written form and alphabet, created by a religious leader in the fifth century A.D., compound the problems of translation. In addition, some words or pronunciations may be understandable only to people of a certain village or mountain valley.

Another language, Georgian, is related to the Caucasian languages and is one of a group that has no connection to any other linguistic group. An even smaller isolated minority is the village of Xinalig in the rugged northern mountains. The village has been isolated since the Middle Ages, and the language spoken by the population of about 1,000 cannot be understood by outsiders.

Baku's Institute of Manuscripts houses many old codices. Experts use the ancient texts to trace the history of Azerbaijan's written scripts.

THE ALPHABET

The written scripts used by Azerbaijanis bear the mark of the external cultural influences that Azerbaijan has been subject to throughout history. In Azerbaijan there are several types of alphabets and scripts that are still in use today. The Arabic script, the Russian Cyrillic alphabet, the modern Azeri alphabet, and the Georgian alphabet are some of the major examples. When the Azerbaijani government made the Azeri Latin script the official alphabet in 1991, Azerbaijanis who had been taught the Cyrillic version had to familiarize themselves with the new script.

AZERI PRONUNCIATION

Azeri words are usually stressed on the last syllable, but the stress is light. There are many regional variations in pronunciation. In some parts of the country, for example, the hard *k* is pronounced more like a *ch*, so that *baki* is pronounced like "ba-chuh" and *seki* is "sha-chee."

Hello	*Salam aleykum*
Good-bye	*Sağ ul*
How are you?	*Necasan?*
Do you speak English?	*Siz ingilizca?*
No. Sorry.	*Xeyr. Bağişla.*
It doesn't matter.	*Bir şey deyil.*
I don't speak Azeri.	*Mən az rbayacan dili danişmiram.*
That's fine! That's great!	*Yaxşidir!*

THE AZERI ALPHABET

Azeri	Roman	Pronunciation
A a	a	long, as in "bar"
B b	b	like the English *b*
C c	c	as in English *j*
Ç ç	ch	as in "chase"
D d	d	like the English *d*
E e	e	as in "bet"
Ə ə	a	short *a*, as in "apple"
F f	f	as in "far"
G g	g	like the *gy* in "Magyar"
Ğ ğ	gh	pronounced at the back of the throat like the French *r*
H h	h	as in "here"
I ı	i	neutral vowel, like the *a* in "ago"
İ i	i	as in "police"
J j	zh	like the *s* in "leisure"
K k	k	as in "kit"
L l	l	as in "let"
M m	m	as in "met"
N n	n	as in "net"
O o	o	short *o* as in "got"
Ö ö	o	like the *e* in "her"
P p	p	as in "pet"
Q q	q	hard *g,* as in "get"
R r	r	a rolled *r*
S s	s	as in "see"
Ş ş	s	as in "shore"
T t	t	as in "toe"
U u	u	as in "chute"
Ü ü	u	like the *ew* in "pew"
V v	v	as in "van"
X x	x	like the *ch* in the Scottish "loch"
Y y	y	as in "yet"
Z z	z	as in "zoo"

ARTS

AZERBAIJAN HAS A RICH TRADITION in each branch of the arts, a tradition that has drawn on both Islamic and European influences. The Islamic presence is evident today in the great architecture of Baku and a few other cities, as well as in early literary forms, especially poetry.

The European influence came later, following the completion of Russia's conquests in 1828. One of the greatest Azeri literary figures, Mirza Fath Ali Akhundzada (1812–78) became central in introducing Western literature and drama. The new literature was concerned with spreading the ideas of the European Enlightenment, with a stress on individual rights and freedoms, gaining knowledge by reason rather than by religious revelation, and the importance of education. These ideas were secular and were designed to reduce the influence of religion.

Innovations in content and form also led to the creation of a new literary language. Based on the sounds and grammar of spoken Azeri, the new language soon replaced Persian as the country's written language. This transformation was enhanced by the publication of a newspaper, called *Akinchi* (*The Plowman*), beginning in 1875.

The early 20th century brought another wave of change to the arts in Azerbaijan. A series of upheavals in Turkey, called the Young Turk Revolution (1908–9), wrenched that country out of a sleepy, conservative past. The aim of the revolt was to create a modern, Western-style country, including the adoption of European styles of clothing, literature, music,

Above: **Azerbaijani artists hard at work on their paintings of the Old Town in Baku.**

Opposite: **Ornate carvings decorate the doors to the Friday Mosque in Baku.**

and other elements of culture. In Azerbaijan the intelligentsia, who were mostly based in Baku, became the leaders in developing the nation's more modern forms of literature and art.

LITERATURE

The different kinds and phases of literary expression in Azerbaijan—folktales, classical Islamic poetry, and modern literature—are considered outstanding examples of the creativity of the Turkish peoples. The poetry of Nezami for example, is regarded as among the finest ever written in the Persian language.

Opposite: **A sculpture of Nezami, the most revered literary figure in Azerbaijan.**

Below: **The Nezami Museum of Literature in Baku houses the manuscripts of Azerbaijan's greatest writers and poets.**

Nezami, who is also known as Ganjavi after his place of birth, Gäncä, wrote in the 12th century. In rhyming couplets, he produced long dramatic tales of love and heroism. His most famous epic, called *Khamseh* (*The Quintuplet*), consisted of five romantic masterpieces: *Khosrow and Shirin*, *The Treasury of Mysteries*, *The Story of Leyli and Majnum*, *The Seven Beauties*, and *The Book of Alexander the Great*. Almost every town in Azerbaijan has a statue of Nezami, and there is often a street named after him as well.

Modern Azeri literature emerged in the 19th century, following the Russian conquest. Even the greatest of the new writers, Mirza Fath Ali Akhundzada, was influenced by the insightful writing of Nezami. Akhundzada introduced drama in the mid-1800s, believing that this was the best way to convey ideas to a public that was largely illiterate. He wrote biting satires, exposing the social ills of the times.

Two followers of Akhundzada—Najaf bay Vazirov and Abdurrahman Haqverdiev—introduced tragic dramas. By the early 1900s, professional theater had become a major form of public entertainment. Azerbaijani literature and theater also influenced Turkey and other countries. During this flowering of the country's culture, the first Azerbaijani opera, *Leyli and*

Majnun, based on the poem by Nezami, added a vital new element to the country's arts.

Magazines and newspapers also multiplied in the early 1900s. One of the most popular publications was a satirical journal called *Mollah Nasroddin*. Another journal, *Fuyuzat* (*Bliss*), championed the romantic idea that all Turkic-speaking peoples could be united.

THE SOVIET PERIOD

The period of Soviet rule that began in 1921 created major changes in Azeri literature and the arts. The communist campaign for literacy produced a new generation of readers. At the same time, however, Soviet dictator Josef Stalin was ruthless in suppressing dissent. Some of the most talented Azeri writers were persecuted, and their books were banned. Artistic talent declined with a new emphasis on "Soviet realism," novels and

COMIC WISDOM

The satiric journal *Mollah Nasroddin* was named after the most popular comic figure in western Asia and the Middle East. The character of Mollah Nasroddin dates back to the Middle Ages and survives today in various literary guises, as well as in comic strips and popular jokes. Nasroddin typifies the wise fool, a figure who seems silly and clownlike, but whose words always contain wisdom or a special logic.

Here is a typical Nasroddin story: Mollah Nasroddin had lost his keys, and a friend found him on the floor searching for the keys.

"Do you know where you lost them?" the friend asked.

"Oh, yes," the mollah answered. "Outside in the yard."

"Well, why are you looking here in the house?"

"Because the light's much better in here."

stories depicting the triumph of the workers over the hated capitalists. All forms of literary expression were suppressed by Stalin's government. In the period just before the 1921 Soviet takeover, 63 newspapers and magazines were in circulation. All but a handful were forced to stop publication, although several moved underground.

The library at the Palace of Culture in Baku. Before the 1980s, literature and the arts in Azerbaijan were severely restricted by Soviet censorship.

The late 1980s witnessed a sharp change in Soviet control when Mikhail Gorbachev introduced the policy of glasnost. Writers whose works had been banned saw their creations and their reputations restored. This was accompanied by a great literary revival in which young men and women once again feverishly produced poetry, novels, short fiction, drama, and a variety of journals and magazines.

Since independence, Azeri literature has benefited from increased contact with the West. The greatest difficulty now is the lack of financial support. Soviet control had taken away freedom, but it had provided financial security.

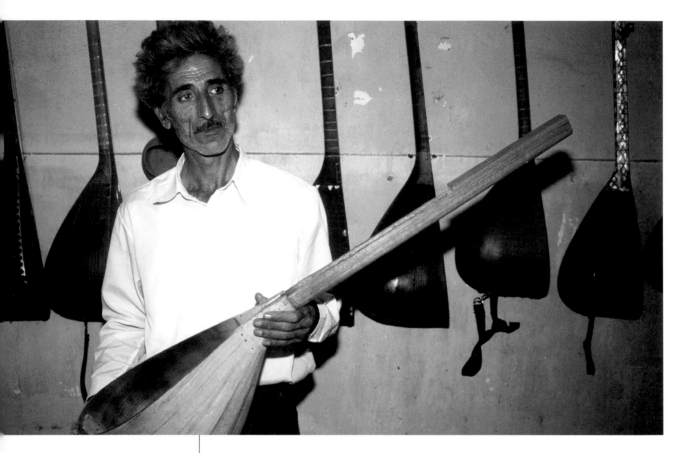

A craftsman displays one of Azerbaijan's traditional musical instruments, the *saz*.

MUSIC AND DANCE

As in many art forms, Azerbaijani music builds on folk traditions that reach back nearly 1,000 years. Traveling poet/singers, called *ashugs*, made their living by performing at weddings and public functions. In poetry and song, they recounted the deeds of ancient heroes, usually strumming a stringed instrument called a *kobuz*.

The *ashugs* often competed with one another in contests that were much like the competitions held among wandering poets in medieval Europe. The Azerbaijani contests rewarded improvisation in both words and music, and this led to a musical form called *mugam*, a style that is still popular today. Like jazz, *mugam* is varied, with different forms used to convey different feelings or moods. An echo of the *ashugs* is found in *mugam* song cycles with texts based on classical poetry.

Mugam also refers to the traditional trio that performs the music. Most *mugams* consist of a singer, a *kamancha* player, and a *tar* player. Both the *tar* and the *kamancha* are stringed instruments. The *tar* has a keyhole-shaped opening, and the strings are plucked. The *kamancha* has a round opening and its strings are made of horsehair or silk; the sounding board is made of gazelle hide. Public performances of *mugam* are a popular form of entertainment, and clever improvisations receive the most enthusiastic applause.

Traditional Azeri musicians entertain diners at a restaurant in Baku.

Jazz became popular late in the Baku oil-boom days, an import from the United States in the 1920s. In the 1950s, a jazz pianist from Baku named Vagif Mustafazade began mixing *mugam* improvisations with jazz elements to produce a new sound called *mugam* jazz. His daughter Aziza has continued to develop *mugam* jazz and her CDs—combined with European tours—have won her an international following.

As in music, folk traditions in dance remain extremely popular. Tours by professional groups and performances by local amateur groups are still the most popular forms of public entertainment.

The music, the costumes, and the dance forms are stylized re-creations of ancient traditions. *Lesginka*, for example, is a popular dance developed in the Middle Ages among the Lezghian people in the northern mountains. The dance begins with a man performing a solo, wearing the costume of a mountain warrior and often brandishing a sword. A woman enters, and the male dances to attract her with concise steps and forceful arm movements. The woman dances quietly around him until he finally wins her over. The entire dance takes 10 to 15 minutes and is immediately followed by other short stories in movement.

FOLK ARTS

Azerbaijan shares, with many other western Asian nations, a reputation for great artistic skill in handicrafts. While the country is best known for its handwoven rugs, Azerbaijan's craftspeople also produce outstanding pottery, ceramics, metalwork, and calligraphy.

Most artistic styles and techniques are heavily influenced by Persian and early Islamic art. Since Islamic law banned the artistic depiction of humans, Azeris acquired extraordinary skill in detailed ornamentation and abstract design. Craft workers in Tabrïz became famous for manuscript illumination, applying rich and detailed ornamentation to miniatures.

Azerbaijan is best known for its variety of textiles, including rugs, carpets, shawls, veils, and towels. Small handwoven rugs differ in design from region to region. Dagestan rugs, for example, feature a short wool pile, with weft threads often of cotton. The highly detailed geometric designs create the impression of brightly colored mosaics. Rugs from other regions might include highly stylized images of pheasants, peacocks, flowers, or animals.

Azeri crafts also feature embroidered textiles. They use brightly colored threads—occasionally of gold or silver—as well as tiny beads to create designs on a thin wool fabric called *tirme*. Geometric patterns are common, but brightly colored birds and other animals are also often featured.

Above: **A display of vessels handcrafted in the village of Lahich.**

Opposite: **Azeris still perform folk dances influenced by ancient traditions.**

97

The mysterious Maiden's Tower of Baku.

ARCHITECTURE

Azerbaijan's architecture reflects various styles that have changed throughout history. There are scattered ruins, as well as fragments and artifacts that date back to prehistoric times. There are also relics from the Zoroastrian period and the era of the Roman empire (including graffiti written by a lonely Roman soldier unhappy at being assigned to such a remote outpost).

The most impressive architecture comes from the long Islamic period. Islamic structures include mosques, minarets (the towers from which the muezzin issues the call to prayer five times a day), mausoleums, palaces, karavan-sarays (from the days of the camel caravans), and madrassas (centers of Islamic learning).

One of the most famous buildings is the Maiden's Tower in Baku. This sturdy oval-shaped fortress is eight stories high, with stairways carved into the thick walls. It was started as a defensive tower in the seventh or eighth century and completed in the 12th century. No one knows exactly how the structure got its name or why a door on the third floor opens onto thin air.

Baku's walled Old Town contains other architectural wonders, including the 15th-century Palace of the Shirvanshahs, which was carefully restored in 2003. The mansions of the 19th-century oil barons are favorite tourist attractions, even though some of the buildings are in poor repair. Baku's subway stations, built during the Soviet period, are considered the most successful examples of communist-style architecture. Other Soviet buildings were usually

massive concrete public buildings and imposing blocks of apartment buildings. Some Soviet buildings have been partially submerged by the rising waters of the Caspian Sea.

RADIO, TELEVISION, AND FILM

Throughout the Soviet period, radio, television, and film were controlled by the government. As a result, programming tended to be little more than communist propaganda, emphasizing the workers' heroic struggle against capitalism. Azeri filmmakers became famous for their documentaries, which seemed to be able to sidestep a heavy propagandistic tone.

Since independence, programmers and filmmakers have struggled to find their directions. A handful of films has done well, including *The Bat*, which won the 1995 Grand Prix at the International Film Festival in Angers, France. In spite of these successes, the Azeri film industry has not yet lived up to the potential that film critics predicted. Movie theaters show mostly old Russian films or American films dubbed in Russian.

The Palace of the Khans in Sheki is another of Azerbaijan's historic monuments. Inside, beautiful murals inspired by the writing of Nezami adorn the palace walls.

LEISURE

THE PEOPLE OF AZERBAIJAN are family oriented, and leisure time is usually family time. The pace is generally relaxed and easygoing. Evenings are often spent outdoors, talking, playing chess or *nard*, or, as rural villagers like to say, "just watching the world go by."

Urban dwellers enjoy evening and weekend strolls, often through the Old Town of Baku or other cities. The main shopping areas are pedestrianized, enabling people to walk and talk without traffic concerns. For shopping, some Azerbaijanis prefer the Soviet-era department stores, which provide low-cost one-stop shopping. Every city and town also offers a wide variety of craft shops for items such as carpets, embroidery, copperware, and ceramics. Baku's shopping center includes designer stores with luxury items from Paris, Rome, London, and New York.

Except in Baku, Azerbaijani families do not go out to dinner often. Still, restaurants are great gathering places for social occasions such as weddings, birthdays, and holidays. Family and friends are likely to spend several hours at a festive meal, often accompanied by loud music. Wedding feasts are probably the favorite social event.

Throughout the country, most Azeris' relations with locals and foreigners alike are friendly. As more and more foreigners discover this ruggedly beautiful country, families often open their homes to overnight guests when tourist facilities are not available. For the visitors, a warm cottage with brightly colored rugs, accompanied by tea and *ktap* (pastry filled with cheese and herbs), offer a delightful introduction to Azerbaijan.

Above: **Having tea with friends and playing *nard* are some of the leisure activities Azerbaijanis indulge in.**

Opposite. **A well-coiffed Azerbaijani woman browses through the racks of an upscale Western-style clothing store in Baku.**

101

SEASONAL ACTIVITIES

Azerbaijan has great potential as an inviting place for outdoor activities. It possesses spectacular scenery, and its towering mountains and rugged hills are ideal for skiing. The Caspian Sea's long coastline makes it ideal for summer sports. Since Azerbaijanis gained independence, however, they have been slow to take advantage of the possibilities, largely because of the warfare and economic upheaval that overshadowed much of the 1990s.

A number of obstacles have to be overcome in order for the country to develop its recreational facilities. There is a growing interest in skiing, for example, but there are few facilities, and these tend to have antiquated equipment and poorly maintained slopes. In 2004 several European companies began preliminary planning for ski resorts in the Caucasus Mountains.

There are obstacles when it comes to summer activities, too. Swimming in the Caspian Sea is popular, but the beaches in the region of the Abseron Peninsula suffer from serious oil pollution and inadequately treated industrial and municipal sewage. Beaches north or south of the peninsula attract more people. Pollution also limits water sports such as sailing, boating, and waterskiing, and some people say they do not like the obstacle course created by oil derricks.

Hiking, mountaineering, and hunting continue to be popular activities. Although Azerbaijan has several snowcapped peaks, there are few approaches for climbers. However, hiking through the rugged hills and mountains attracts a growing number of foreign visitors as well as locals. Many hikers hire local villagers to guide them through mountain passes.

Hunting in groups can become an elaborate affair for Azerbaijanis and foreign workers who can afford it. Often on horseback or in four-wheel-drive vehicles, a hunting group will include a guide, a cook, and equipment managers for tours that wind through the rough foothills or

Opposite: **Polluted coastal waters keep most swimmers and sun worshipers away but not this Azerbaijani man.**

Below: **Hikers tracking up Babadag, a mountain in Azerbaijan.**

up into the mountains. The hunters are often seeking trophies, such as wild boars or eastern Caucasian ibex (mountain goats with huge horns). Most guides are careful to avoid endangered species such as Persian gazelles or striped hyenas.

RESORTS

During the Soviet era, Azerbaijan had numerous vacation resorts called sanatoriums. These were state-run facilities where workers from factories throughout the Soviet Union could come for a week or two of rest and recreation. There were also less elaborate vacation places called *turbazas*. These usually consisted of clusters of cabins in forest areas or near a lake. Both sanatoriums and *turbazas* were often built next to natural hot springs.

A hot spring at the resort town of Masalli Istisu.

A number of these vacation areas are still in use. The best ones now operate as private clubs, or are run by government agencies, such as the ministry of defense. Others, especially the *turbazas*, have become resorts where Azerbaijanis can rent space for a summer or winter vacation.

BOARD GAMES

Many Azerbaijanis are fascinated by two of the world's most ancient board games: chess and *nard*. Both games are played by all ages, and it is said that kids would rather play *nard* than watch television.

CHESS In 1985 Baku native Garry Kasparov became, at 22, the youngest world chess champion in history. Kasparov remained champion until 2000, when he lost to Russian Vladimir Kramnik. In his 15 years as world champion, the only time Kasparov lost a match was in 1997 when he was beaten by an IBM computer nicknamed Deep Blue.

Kasparov's amazing record and his bold style of play have heightened the great popularity of chess among Azerbaijanis of all ages. A young woman named Ilaha Gadimova could be the next hard-to-beat chess player. When she was 12, she won the country's 16-year-old division and has gone on to win other national and international championships.

Chess grandmaster Garry Kasparov was born in Baku in 1963.

Elderly Azerbaijani men engaged in a match of *nard*. *Nard* is the oldest board game in existence and is by far the most popular game in Azerbaijan.

NARD The board game called *nard*, or backgammon, is even more popular than chess and can probably be considered the nation's favorite recreational activity. The object of this two-player game is to move your pieces through the four parts of the board before your opponent does. Although the number of spaces moved depends on a roll of the dice, the game is an exciting combination of luck and skill. Each player, for example, can block the other or can force an opponent's game piece back to the start.

People of all ages can spend hours playing *nard* and practicing new strategies. In every café there are bound to be several pairs of people playing the game, usually while they have their tea and jam. It is not unusual for a foreign visitor to be invited to play *nard* even if he or she does not speak a word of Azeri.

INTERNATIONAL COMPETITION

When Azerbaijani athletes are engaged in international competition, they give the nation a chance to express its tremendous pride. In 1996, for example, 23 athletes traveled to Atlanta, Georgia, for the Summer Olympic Games. This was the first independent Azerbaijani Olympic team, and the athletes were treated as national heroes, especially when wrestler Namig Abdullayev won a silver medal. (Abdullayev was to go on to win a gold medal in the Olympic Games in 2000.)

International competition, including several European championships, has also provided a unique opportunity for women. Some women, such as Zulfiya Huseynova, have chosen unusual sports. She became world champion in sumo wrestling in 1995 and 1996 and European champion in 1997. Similarly, Zemfira Meftaheddinova has been a champion in shooting, both in team and individual competition.

The Azerbaijani government has encouraged participation in international competition by establishing a sports complex in Zagulta to provide

Farid Mansurov of Azerbaijan grapples with his Swedish competitor in a Greco-Roman wrestling match at the Summer Olympics of 2004. Like Namig Abdullayev, Mansurov was to also take home the Olympic gold medal.

advanced training. By the late 1990s, 165 Azerbaijani athletes were participating in international and European competitions, winning 22 gold medals, in total, in the European championships.

RURAL SPORTS

In 1994 the government created the ministry for youth and sport. The ministry promotes "physical training" in schools. All colleges and universities now have physical-training departments. In rural areas, the ministry has placed emphasis on national sports. These include *chougan*, a game on horseback similar to polo, and *gyulash*, a traditional form of wrestling.

Team games for secondary-school-aged students are also popular. A favorite springtime game is "cockfight," in which two teams face each other in a circle about 12 feet (3.7 m) in diameter. With hands on their waists, the members of one team stand on their left legs, while their opponents perch on their right legs. After a signal is given, each team tries to force the other out of the circle, while keeping their hands on their waists and one leg in the air.

"Seven beauties" is a game for girls. Seven girls, each equipped with a crochet hook and

colored threads compete to crochet stockings. The winner is the one who is judged both the fastest and the most skilled.

SOCCER

As in most countries of the world, soccer is immensely popular. Kids of all ages play it in casual pickup games as well as in soccer clubs and at secondary schools.

The national soccer team is a source of great national pride. In October 2004, the Azerbaijani team traveled to England for a World Cup match. Even though the Azerbaijani players lost by a score of 1 to 0, they proved they could compete with the best in the world.

Left: **Soccer is an especially popular sport in Azerbaijan.**

Opposite: ***Gyulash* is a traditional sport that is similar to Greco-Roman wrestling,**

FESTIVALS

BOTH RELIGIOUS AND SECULAR holidays are celebrated in Azerbaijan. Religious festivals are taken seriously, even though many Muslims practice Islam very loosely.

Many secular celebrations are occasions for demonstrating pride in Azerbaijan's short history as a democratic republic. These gatherings feature marching bands, waving flags, military displays, and speeches.

Left: **A political rally in Baku. Rallies like these provide opportunities for Azerbaijanis to celebrate their hard-won nationhood.**

Opposite: **An Azerbaijani boy dressed in his new year's best. Novruz Bayrami is the traditional New Year's Day for Azerbaijan and other western Asian countries, such as Iran and Afghanistan.**

THE NEW YEAR

A springtime festival called Novruz Bayrami is held on March 20 and 21. It marks the beginning of the new year according to the ancient Persian solar calendar. This is the traditional time for families to spring-clean their homes. People even cleanse their souls by jumping over bonfires. Sprouts of wheat and barley are grown to welcome the new crop year, and special rice dishes are also prepared.

THE FESTIVAL OF SACRIFICE

Islamic celebrations run the emotional gamut from joyful to solemn to tragic or dramatic. The Festival of Sacrifice, called Gurban Bayrami, is held in the spring of the year, in either February or March, according to the Islamic calendar. This festival celebrates an episode in the life of the patriarch Abraham, one of the most revered figures in Judaism, Christianity, and Islam. His faith was tested on Mount Moriah, when God ordered him to sacrifice his son Isaac.

Azeri families celebrate the festival, especially in rural areas, by ritually slaughtering a sheep. The sheep, a symbol of patriarch Abraham's sacrifice, is then given to the poor and also shared among friends and family, becoming the basis for a great feast. The celebration is much the same in urban areas.

AŞURA

This Shiite holy day is held in early spring, following the Islamic lunar calendar. The day commemorates the martyrdom of Husayn ibn'Ali, the grandson of Prophet Muhammad, who was killed at the Battle of Karbala in A.D. 680.

In the historic event, Husayn and his family were traveling to Al-Kufa, where he expected to be crowned caliph. Instead, he was met by an opposition army. In a brief battle, Husayn and all his followers were killed.

Since that event, the 10th day of Muharram has been observed as a time of mourning by Shiite Muslims. They consider the tomb of the decapitated

Left: **Shiite Muslims resting in a mosque after a ritual march mourning the death of Husayn ibn'Ali on Aşura.**

Opposite: **As part of the celebration of Novruz Bayrami, this girl is choosing the wheat sprouts that will decorate her home. To Azerbaijanis, the young sprouts symbolize rebirth and new beginnings.**

Husayn in Karbala to be the holiest place in the world. Passion plays reenact the tragedy. In some processions, men of all ages, dressed in black, beat their chests and flail themselves with metal blades to relieve Husayn's suffering. This practice continues, even though government and religious leaders discourage it.

RAMADAN

This month-long fast occurs in the ninth month of the Islamic calendar, in usually October or November. It was originally held at the same time as the Jewish Day of Atonement but then evolved into a separate event

During Ramadan Muslims worldwide end each day of fasting with a meal with family and friends.

to distinguish it as a time of obedience rather than reparation. During Ramadan, Muslims are to refrain from eating, drinking, and smoking from dawn to dusk.

At the end of each fast during Ramadan, people tend to feast with family and friends far into the night. A special festival, ïd al-Fiṭr, marks the end of Ramadan with food, music, prayers, and an exchange of presents.

NATIONAL HOLIDAYS

January 1	New Year's Day
January 20	Martyrs' Day
March 8	International Women's Day
May 28	Republic Day
June 15	National Salvation Day
June 26	Armed Forces Day
October 18	National Independence Day
November 12	Constitution Day
November 17	National Revival Day
December 31	Solidarity Day

PATRIOTIC CELEBRATIONS

The great pride the Azerbaijani people feel in their independent republic is evident in the many patriotic holidays. Some of these holidays celebrate the country's first brief episode of independence. Republic Day, for example, honors the founding of the first Azerbaijani Democratic Republic in 1918, and Armed Forces Day celebrates the creation of the republic's first army in the same year.

Other patriotic days commemorate declaring independence in 1991 and establishing the new republic. National Revival Day, on November 17,

Azerbaijanis celebrate their independence from the Soviet Union which was declared on August 30, 1991, just 12 days after the Azerbaijani republic was formed.

marks the first anti-Soviet uprising in 1988. More than two years of uprisings and repression followed. One milepost on the road to independence came in 1989 when Azerbaijanis and Iranians tore down the border fences the Soviets had put up between the two countries to prevent the Iranian Azerbaijanis from joining the northern Azeris. This event is celebrated as Solidarity Day on December 31 each year.

Soviet repression is marked by Martyrs' Day, on January 20, which is a tribute to civilians in Baku who were gunned down by Soviet troops in 1990. October 18 celebrates National Independence Day, marking the day in 1991 when the parliament announced the dissolution of the Soviet Union, and Azerbaijan began its second democratic republic.

After declaring independence, the new government was not able to settle the bitter warfare with Armenians over Nagorno-Karabakh. In 1993 Heydar Aliyev took advantage of the chaos and was named president. On June 15 parliament officially asked Aliyev to lead the country, a date that is now celebrated as National Salvation Day. Constitution Day (November 12) commemorates the adoption of the republic's new constitution in 1995.

A BUSINESS FESTIVAL

Possibly the largest annual event in Azerbaijan is the Caspian Oil and Gas Show. Held in late May or early June in and around Baku, this week-long event brings people together from all over the world. The Oil and Gas Show has become a festive celebration of Azerbaijan's potential to return to its position as one of the great producers of oil and natural gas. Unlike the late 1800s, however, there is now a strong emphasis on environmental protection, including the restoration of fisheries and the protection of safe nesting places for birds.

The Caspian Oil and Gas Show is a major event in Azerbaijan.

117

FOOD

AZERBAIJAN IS KNOWN for its rich variety of foods. To a great extent, this variety reflects the many different foods that can be grown in the republic's several climatic zones. Colder regions, for example, provide outstanding grapes and many kinds of nuts as well as staples such as wheat and barley. Subtropical areas produce pomegranates and citrus fruit. The Azerbaijani people have also been very creative in their use of herbs and spices to vary standard dishes. They also make use of several wild plants, some of which are not known in other countries.

Even with Azerbaijan's variety of foods and flavors, one thing is constant—a heavy reliance on kebabs, especially those made with lamb. The kebab is the main dish at most family dinners, and it is often referred to by the Russian word *shashlik*, meaning "sword." The standard kebab consists of chunks of meat threaded onto a skewer and grilled over the embers. Unlike American cookouts, the vegetables are usually grilled on a separate skewer. The *lüla* kebab is made of chopped meat, spices, and herbs that are shaped into little balls and then grilled on skewers. The country's cuisine is in the process of a major change. The long period of Soviet rule had a profound impact on the foods people ate and on the country's agricultural products. The Azerbaijani people are deciding which Russian foods they want to discard and which they want to incorporate into a new national cuisine for the 21st century.

Above: **A waiter presents skewers of kebab to the delight of diners in an Azerbaijani restaurant.**

Opposite: **These market stalls in Baku are well stocked with grain and other staples.**

TRADITIONAL FAVORITES

While the lamb kebab is the most common main dish, there are several other specialties in Azerbaijan.

DOLMA There are several varieties of *dolma*, all of them with unique flavors. The basic recipe consists of minced lamb mixed with rice and flavored with mint, fennel, and cinnamon. The mixture is then wrapped in grape leaves to make *yarpaq dolmasi* or wrapped in cabbage leaves to make *kalam dolmasi*. Restaurants often serve tomatoes, green peppers, or eggplants stuffed with *dolma*.

SOUPS AND STEWS Azeris are fond of hot and cold soups, including dishes that are thick enough to be called stews. *Dovga*, for example, is a hot thick soup made of yogurt, rice, spinach, and fennel. *Dograma* is a cold soup of sour milk, potato, onion, and cucumber.

Piti is more a stew than a soup. It is made of lamb, fat, chickpeas, and saffron. Like many Azeri dishes, *piti* is cooked and served in individual earthenware crocks.

Dushbara is a classic dish consisting of small ravioli-size dumplings stuffed with minced lamb and herbs, served in a hot broth.

PLOV This is one of the standard dishes, consisting of lamb, rice, chopped onion, and prunes. Saffron and cinnamon are added to this flavorful dish, which is commonly made in people's homes but hard to find in restaurants.

BALIG *Balig* is a popular fish dish. The fish, usually sturgeon, is cut into chunks and grilled like a kebab. It is served with a tangy sour-plum sauce.

LAVANGI Lavangi is one of many outstanding regional specialties consisting of a chicken stuffed with walnuts and herbs and then baked in an earthenware casserole. It is a specialty of the Talysh.

Above: **Balig is the traditional Azerbaijani equivalent of fish kebabs.**

Opposite: **A plate of dolma.**

THE SOVIET INFLUENCE

During Azerbaijan's 70 years as one of the 15 Soviet republics, the central government in Moscow had a strong influence on the foods the Azerbaijanis ate and produced. This influence continues today as the people struggle to re-establish a national cuisine.

Soviet planners hoped to transform the many nationalities and cultures that made up its vast empire into a single efficient system. Each republic or province would contribute one or more important products to the national economy. Azerbaijan, for instance, was a major oil producer, and its farms provided slightly more than 10 percent of the fruit and vegetables

Azeri men selling melons along the roadside. In the Soviet era, Azerbaijan was a major supplier of fruit and vegetables to the entire Soviet bloc.

needed for the entire Soviet Union. Other republics, in turn, sent certain products to Azerbaijan: butter came from Russia, poultry from Hungary, condensed milk from the Ukraine, and cheese from Bulgaria.

Another way that communist planners influenced national cuisine was by encouraging people to follow a typical Russian diet. Throughout Azerbaijan, workers in factories and government offices and students in universities and vocational schools all ate in large government-operated cafés. The food was somewhat bland, but it was wholesome and it was free. While a few national dishes, such as lamb kebabs, were served, the menu emphasized traditional Russian foods, such as goulash, meat cutlets, *shi* (fish soup), and borscht. This seemed to be part of the communist plan to forge a single, united Soviet people.

Harvesting wheat at an Azerbaijani state farm in 1947.

Even today, more than a decade after Azerbaijan gained its independence, many traditional Russian dishes seem to have become part of the emerging Azerbaijani cuisine. A basic Russian salad, for example, made of beans, potatoes, carrots, pickled beets, and cabbage, is now standard in many Azerbaijani homes. Another Russian dish is called *stolichniy*; it is basically a potato salad with shredded chicken, carrots, and peas, topped with a mayonnaise-like dressing. This has become a popular first dish at weddings and other large functions.

Desserts have also been changed by the Soviet experience. In the past, Azerbaijani families enjoyed one or two national desserts, usually pastries like baklava. Baklava is still popular, but Russian cafés introduced cakes and, around the time of World War II, ice cream. Both cake and ice cream are now standard.

An Azerbaijani mother treats her child to American fast food in one of two McDonald's restaurants in Baku.

FAST FOODS

Even fast foods reflect the years of Soviet influence. At inexpensive snack bars called *yemakxanos*, or food houses, people could buy quick Russian foods like *pirozhki*, a dough stuffed with potatoes, pears, and rice or meat. Another standby was *blinchiki*, a pancake stuffed with cheese or meat. By the end of the Soviet era, *yemakxanos* were found in every city neighborhood and in every town and village. Traditional Azeri foods were also popular.

European and American fast foods such as hamburgers and hot dogs, have now been added to the Azerbaijani diet. Two sleek new McDonald's in Baku draw large crowds, but it may be too early to tell how popular they will be when the novelty wears off.

ALCOHOL

In traditional Azeri Muslim families, adults used to drink modest amounts of locally produced wine and beer. But alcohol was not often served at parties or in restaurants. As with food, the Soviet period led to changes in Azerbaijani patterns. The use of alcohol, including vodka, became commonplace, and today alcohol is served freely at wedding parties and other functions, as well as in restaurants. In addition, Azerbaijan became a major producer of wines for export, ranging from inexpensive table varieties, such as Aghdam, to fine red and white wines.

CHANGING TASTES

Since gaining independence, many Azerbaijanis have been eager to throw off Soviet influence and re-establish a more traditional national cuisine. The government has reduced its role in economic planning, and farm families are encouraged to try new crops and livestock to test the demand for different types of food.

While many favorite foods—kebabs, *dolma*, *balig*, and a host of other dishes—have remained popular through the Soviet era, a few traditions seem to have disappeared for good. Street vendors used to serve a warm drink called *saalab*. *Saalab* was a thick beverage made from milk and the root of the wild *saalab* plant. Vendors kept it warm in a samovar. The convenience of tea, coffee, and other fast-food drinks seems to account for *saalab*'s decline in popularity.

In a similar way, a traditional bread called *takhta* may have disappeared because it was simply too troublesome to make. The bread was as hard as wood—in fact, *takhta* is the Azeri word for "board"—but it was popular throughout the country, especially with merchants who made long overland journeys. Once the takhta was soaked in hot water or broth, it became sweet and tasty. Today there are no slow-moving caravans crossing the plains, and modern truckers have found more convenient substitutes.

In addition to traditional Azeri favorites, the emerging national cuisine borrows freely from the foods of other countries. Dishes from Turkey, Iran, and some of the central Asian republics have slowly been added to the standard family menu. The most visible signs of international flavors are found in Azerbaijan's restaurants.

EATING OUT

For most Azerbaijani families, dining out is reserved for special occasions when a large group of family members and friends book

Azerbaijanis, in general, do not have a habit of eating out.

an entire restaurant, or part of it, for a long meal. Loud music is common as is belly dancing.

The republic's cities offer a wide range of foreign restaurants. Baku, of course, leads the international parade with Turkish, American, Italian, French, Chinese, Japanese, Thai, Indian, and Mexican restaurants. Azerbaijani eateries continue to be the most popular.

SHASHLIK (LAMB KEBAB)

This recipe serves four.

1 large grated onion
1 tablespoon lemon juice
1 tablespoon olive oil
1 teaspoon salt
$\frac{1}{4}$ teaspoon black pepper
2 pounds boneless lamb (leg
    or shoulder cut), cut into 1- to
    $1\frac{1}{2}$-inch cubes
2 medium onions, cut into
    $\frac{1}{4}$-inch-thick chunks
2 fresh tomatoes, cut into wedges
10–12 scallions, trimmed
1 lemon wedge

Make a marinade in a large mixing bowl by combining the grated onion, lemon juice, olive oil, salt, and pepper. Mix thoroughly. Add the lamb cubes and let them marinate for at least three hours (at room temperature). Stir the ingredients every hour or so. In a charcoal broiler or on a grill, let the briquettes burn until a white ash appears on the surface. If necessary, use a kitchen broiler heated to its highest point. String the cubed lamb onto four skewers, alternating the meat with the chunks of onion. Press the pieces together. Broil about 4 inches (10 cm) from the heat source. Turn the skewers occasionally, until the lamb is well done (about 15 minutes). Slide the lamb and onions off the skewers onto warmed plates. Serve with the tomatoes, scallions, and lemon wedges.

RICE PILAF WITH FRUIT AND NUTS

This recipe serves four.

2 tablespoons dried currants
4 medium-sized dried prunes,
    pitted and cut into strips
4 tablespoons butter
1/4 cup dried apricot, cut into
    strips
1/4 cup finely chopped blanched
    untoasted almonds
1 tablespoon honey
1 cup long-grain unconverted
    rice
2 cups of water

In a bowl of warm water, soak the currants and prunes for 15 minutes. Remove and pat them dry on paper towels. Melt the butter in a casserole over high heat and add the apricots, currants, prunes, and almonds. Reduce the heat to low and cook uncovered for 3 to 5 minutes, or until the nuts are lightly browned. Stir in the honey and rice, cover with the water, and bring to a boil over high heat. Reduce the heat to low, cover the casserole, and simmer for 25 minutes, or until the water has been absorbed. Serve hot as a side dish with lamb or poultry. This can also be a main dish for lunch or a light supper.

PARCHA DOSHAMYA PLOV (LAMB WITH DRIED FRUITS AND WALNUTS)

2 tablespoons butter

2 pounds lamb (boneless or shoulder cut), cut into 1 to 1¹/₂-inch cubes

1 small onion, chopped

¹/₂ cup dried apricots, cut into pieces

¹/₂ cup raisins

¹/₂ cup walnuts, chopped (chestnuts can also be used)

1¹/₂ cups beef broth

¹/₂ teaspoon caraway seeds

a few threads of saffron, ground salt and pepper to taste

2 cups rice

2 teaspoons cinnamon

Melt 1 tablespoon of butter in a heavy pot. Add the lamb and brown it. Add the onion, dried fruit, nuts, broth, caraway seeds, saffron, and salt and pepper. Bring to a boil over high heat. Reduce the heat to very low and simmer uncovered for at least 1 hour, until the lamb is cooked and tender. Add water if necessary. In a separate pot, cook the rice according to the directions on the package. Melt the second tablespoon of butter. Place the rice on a serving plate and spoon the stew on top. Pour the melted butter over the *plov* and sprinkle with cinnamon.

SALAD WITH SMOKED SALMON

4 eggs, hard-boiled
2 ounces smoked salmon or tuna
1 cucumber
1 tomato
4–6 scallions
2 cups lettuce or mixed salad greens
salad dressing (oil and vinegar)

Most Azeri dinners begin with a salad. While tomatoes, cucumbers, and onions are the most common ingredients, this salad adds both smoked salmon and hard-boiled eggs for flavor. (Tuna fish can be substituted for the salmon.)

Cut the cooked eggs in half lengthwise. Remove part of the yolks and replace with pieces of smoked salmon. Slice the cucumber, tomato, and scallions. Place the salad greens, cucumber, tomato slices, and eggs on individual plates. Crumble the rest of the egg yolks on top and sprinkle with the sliced scallions. Add salad dressing to taste.

OVSHALA (ROSE-PETAL DRINK)

This recipe serves three to five.

5 cups water
petals from three roses in full bloom
¹/₂ teaspoon lemon juice
3 tablespoons sugar

Although bottled or canned soft drinks are becoming increasingly popular, many rural Azerbaijanis still make a beverage called *sharbat* by simply mixing almost any fruit with boiling water. Try this *sharbat* variation called *ovshala*. Boil the water. Add the rose petals and lemon juice. Turn off the heat and let the mixture stand at least 6 hours or overnight. Drain into a pitcher. Discard the rose petals. Add the sugar and stir. Chill in the refrigerator and serve cold.

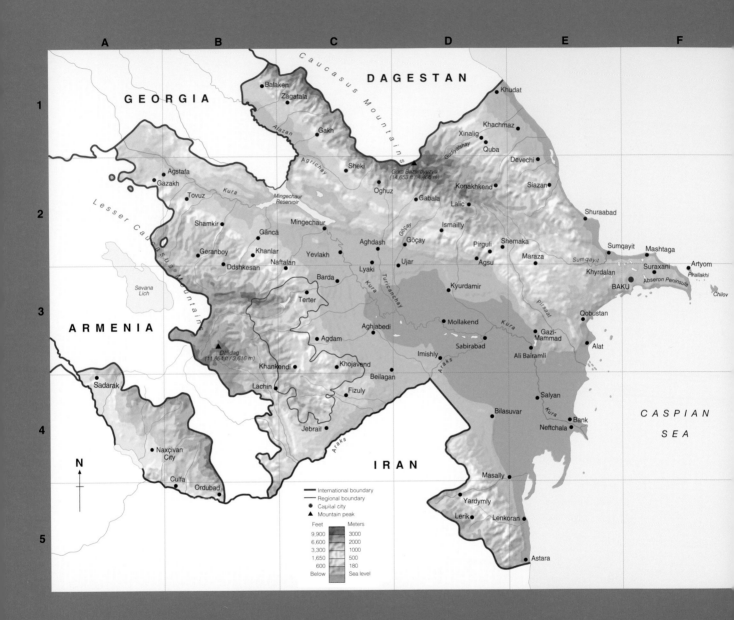

GEORGIA

DAGESTAN

Caucasus Mountains

1
Balaken
Zagatala
Gakh
Alazan
Agrichay
Sheki
Oghuz
Gora Bazardyuzyu
(14,653 ft / 4,466 m)
Khudat
Khachmaz
Xinalig
Quba
Gudiyalshay
Devechi
Konakhkend
Siazan

Agstafa
Gazakh
Tovuz
Kura
Mingechaur
Reservoir
Gabala
Lalic
Shuraabad

2
Shamkir
Gäncä
Mingechaur
Aghdash
Göçay
Göçay
Ismailly
Pirguli
Shemaka
Sumqayit
Mashtaga
Geranboy
Khanlar
Naftalan
Yevlakh
Lyaki
Ujar
Agsu
Maraza
Khyrdalan
Suraxani
Artyom
Pirallakhi
Ddshkesan
Barda
Kura
Turicanchay
Kyurdamir
BAKU
Abseron Peninsula
Chilov

Lesser Caucasus Mountains

Sevana
Lich

Terter
Pirsaat
Qobustan

3
ARMENIA
Agdam
Aghjabedi
Mollakend
Kura
Gazi-
Mammad
Alat
Dalidag
(11,864 ft / 3,616 m)
Sabirabad
Ali Bairamli
Khankendi
Khojavend
Imishly
Araks
Lachin
Beilagan
Fizuly
Salyan
CASPIAN
SEA
Bilasuvar
Kura
Bank

4
Jebrail
Araks
Neftchala

Naxçivan
City

Masally

IRAN
Culfa
Ordubad

International boundary
Regional boundary
Capital city
Mountain peak

Yardymly
Lerik
Lenkoran

Sadarak

Feet   Meters
9,900   3000
6,600   2000
3,300   1000
1,650   500
600   180
Below   Sea level

Astara

N

5

MAP OF AZERBAIJAN

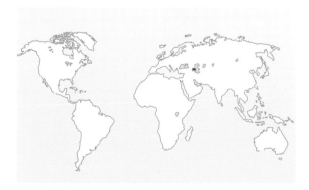

ECONOMIC AZERBAIJAN

Agriculture

- Corn
- Fruit
- Rice
- Silk
- Tea
- Tobacco
- Vineyard

Manufacturing

- Carpet
- Chemicals
- Electrical Goods
- Steel
- Textiles

Services

- Airport
- Port
- Power Station
- Tourism

Natural Resources

- Hydroelectricity
- Limestone
- Oil & Natural Gas

ABOUT THE ECONOMY

GROSS DOMESTIC PRODUCT
US$26.3 billion (2003 estimate)

PER CAPITA GDP
US$3,400

GDP BY SECTOR
Agriculture 14.1 percent, industry 45.7 percent, services 40.2 percent

LAND AREA
33,436 square miles (86,600 square km)

AGRICULTURAL PRODUCTS
Cotton, grain, rice, grapes, fish, cattle, chickens, goats, pigs, sheep

INDUSTRIAL PRODUCTS
Oil products, oil-field equipment, steel, iron ore, cement

PROVEN OIL RESERVES
589 million barrels (2002)

INFLATION RATE
4.6 percent (2004 estimate)

CURRENCY
Azerbaijan manat (AZM)
USD 1 = AZM 4,618 (August 2005)

WORKFORCE
5.09 million

WORKFORCE BY SECTOR
Agriculture and forestry 41 percent, industry 7 percent, services 52 percent

UNEMPLOYMENT RATE
1.2 percent (2004 estimate)

MAIN EXPORTS
Oil and gas, machinery, cotton, food products

MAIN IMPORTS
Machinery and equipment, oil products, food products, metals, chemicals

MAIN TRADE PARTNERS
Italy 30.1 percent, Germany 15.5 percent, Czech Republic 10.8 percent, France 8.8 percent, Georgia 7 percent, Russia 4.9 percent, United States 4.2 percent (2002)

MAIN AIRPORT
Baku

MAIN PORT
Baku

EXTERNAL DEBT
$1.832 billion (2004 estimate)

INTERNET SERVICE PROVIDERS
14

CULTURAL AZERBAIJAN

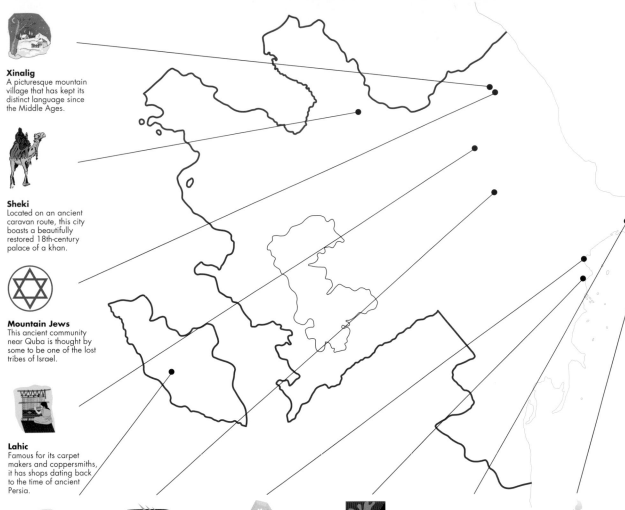

Xinalig
A picturesque mountain village that has kept its distinct language since the Middle Ages.

Sheki
Located on an ancient caravan route, this city boasts a beautifully restored 18th-century palace of a khan.

Mountain Jews
This ancient community near Quba is thought by some to be one of the lost tribes of Israel.

Lahic
Famous for its carpet makers and coppersmiths, it has shops dating back to the time of ancient Persia.

Naxçivan City
According to legend, Naxçivan was founded by the biblical figure Noah before 1500 B.C. Famous for its historic sites.

Observatory
(In the village of Pirguli) This observatory was a major site for Soviet space research in the 1960s and 1970s.

Petroglyphs
More than 6,000 cave engravings have been found near Qobustan. They date to about 10,000 B.C.

Mud Volcanoes
Constantly oozing, these small volcanoes sporadically erupt, sending globs of mud up in the air.

Icari Sahar
This ancient walled city in Baku has narrow cobblestone streets, shops, and ancient mosques.

Ateşgah Fire Temple
Built in the 18th century on the site of an ancient Zoroastrian temple, this temple houses a constant flame that is never extinguished.

ABOUT THE CULTURE

OFFICIAL NAME
Republic of Azerbaijan

CAPITAL
Baku

OTHER MAJOR CITIES
Gäncä, Sumqayit, Shemaka, Quba

FLAG
Divided into three horizontal bars, with blue on top, red in the middle, and green on the bottom. A white crescent and star are in the center of the middle bar.

POPULATION
7,868,385, about 52 percent live in urban areas

POPULATION DENSITY
Approximately 230 people per square mile

ETHNIC GROUPS
Azeris 80 percent, Dagestanis 3.2 percent, Russians 2.5 percent, Armenians 2 percent, Lezghians 2 percent

LIFE EXPECTANCY
75 years for women, 68 years for men

TIME
Azerbaijan is 4 hours ahead of Greenwich Mean Time (GMT + 4). Azerbaijan is 3 hours earlier than Europe and 9 hours earlier than New York.

RELIGIONS
Muslim 93 percent (Shiite 68 percent, Sunni 25 percent); Russian Orthodox, Greek Orthodox, and Armenian Apostolic, about 5 percent; Jews and others, about 2 percent

OFFICIAL LANGUAGE
Azeri

LITERACY RATE
97 percent

EDUCATION
Free and compulsory secondary education

NATIONAL HOLIDAY
National Independence Day (October 18)

LEADERS IN POLITICS
Ayaz N. Mutalibov (president 1991–1992), Abulfaz Elchibey (president 1992–1993), Heydar Aliyev (president 1993–2003), Ilham Aliyev (president since 2003)

LEADERS IN THE ARTS
Mstislav Rostropovich (cellist), Kara Karayev (composer), Samad Vurgun (poet and playwright), Vagif Mustafazade (jazz pianist), Fikrat Amirov (composer)

TIME LINE

IN AZERBAIJAN	IN THE WORLD
753 B.C First human settlements; Stone Age petroglyphs	**753 B.C.** Rome is founded.
400 B.C Caucasian Albania formed; Atropatene in the south	**116–17 B.C.** The Roman Empire reaches its greatest extent, under Emperor Trajan (98–17).
A.D. 200 Atropatene becomes part of Persia.	
A.D. 300–400 Christianity comes to Caucasian Albania.	**A.D. 600** Height of Mayan civilization
A.D. 642 Caucasian Albania becomes Muslim.	**1000** The Chinese perfect gunpowder and begin to use it in warfare.
1110–1200 Seljuk Turkish dynasty	
1236–1498 Mongols of Genghis Khan control Azerbaijan.	
1500 Safavid dynasty; Shiite branch of Islam now official	**1530** Beginning of transatlantic slave trade organized by the Portuguese in Africa.
	1558–1603 Reign of Elizabeth I of England
	1620 Pilgrims sail the *Mayflower* to America.
1722 Safavid rule ends; Azerbaijan is splintered into several khanates.	**1776** U.S. Declaration of Independence
	1789–99 The French Revolution
1804–13 and 1826–28 Two Russo-Persian wars. Russia controls Azerbaijan north of Araks River.	**1861** The U.S. Civil War begins.
	1869 The Suez Canal is opened.
1870–1915 Oil industry makes Baku a boomtown.	**1914** World War I begins.
1918 Azerbaijan forms independent republic.	

IN AZERBAIJAN	IN THE WORLD
1920	
Soviet Red Army invades, ending Azeri independence; Azerbaijan becomes part of the Soviet Union.	
1930s	
Communist purges ordered by Soviet dictator Josef Stalin	**1939**
	World War II begins.
1941–42	
During World War II, German forces invade Russia and reach Greater Caucasus Mountains, but not Azerbaijan.	**1945**
	The United States drops atomic bombs on Hiroshima and Nagasaki.
	1949
	The North Atlantic Treaty Organization (NATO) is formed.
	1957
	The Russians launch Sputnik.
	1966–69
	The Chinese Cultural Revolution
	1986
	Nuclear power disaster at Chernobyl in Ukraine
1991	**1991**
Azerbaijan declares independence from the Soviet Union.	Break-up of the Soviet Union
1992	
War in Nagorno-Karabakh	
1993	
Heydar Aliyev becomes president and wins the October election.	
1994	
Aliyev signs cease-fire with Armenia.	**1997**
	Hong Kong is returned to China.
	2001
	Terrorists crash planes in New York, Washington, D.C., and Pennsylvania.
2003	**2003**
Ilham Aliyev becomes president.	War in Iraq

GLOSSARY

ashugs
Poet-singers in the tradition of strolling minstrels; popular since the Middle Ages.

Beşbarmaq Dâg
Five-Finger Mountain; a place where religious mystics pray and dispense wisdom to their followers.

caviar
The roe of Caspian Sea sturgeons; one of the world's most prized delicacies.

dolgozhiteli
People who have led very long lives.

Icari Sahar
The walled Old Town of Baku.

ïd al-Fiṭr
The feast that marks the end of Ramadan.

intelligentsia
The educated middle class that established the short-lived democratic republic in 1918.

intolerant atheism
Policy implemented by the then Soviet-controlled government, which actively sought to stamp out religious influence on society.

khanate
An area or province ruled by a khan.

Koran
The holy book of Islam.

lesginka
A popular folk dance from the Lezghian peoples of the northern mountains.

madrassa
Islamic center of learning.

mugam
A musical style. Also a trio of musicians that plays in that style.

nard
A hugely popular board game; the same as backgammon.

Pan-Azerbaijani movement
A group whose aim is to unite the northern and southern branches of the Azerbaijani people.

Ramadan
The holiest month in the Islamic calendar. Observant Muslims fast during daylight hours.

shashlik
An Azeri kebab; literally, "sword," in Russian.

zakat
The tax to support the poor; paying this tax is one of the Five Pillars of Islam.

FURTHER INFORMATION

BOOKS

De Waal, Thomas. *Black Garden: Armenia and Azerbaijan through Peace and War*. New York: New York University Press, 2003.

Elliot, Mark. *Azerbaijan with Excursions to Georgia*. London: Trailblazer Publications, 1999.

Goltz, Thomas. *Azerbaijan Diary*. Armonk, NY: M. E. Sharpe, 1998.

Kleveman, Lutz. *The New Great Game: Blood and Oil in Central Asia*. London: Oxford University Press, 1998.

Said, Kurban. *Ali and Nino*. New York: Overlook Press, 1999.

Van der Leeuw, Charles. *Azerbaijan: A Quest for Identity*. New York: Palgrave Macmillan, 2000.

WEB SITES

A to Z of Azerbaijan. www.azerb.com

Azerbaijan International. www.azer.com

Bakupages. www.bakupages.com

Central Intelligence Agency World Factbook (select Azerbaijan from the country list). www.cia.gov/cia/publications/factbook/index.html

Embassy of Azerbaijan in Washington, D.C. www.azembassy.com

Lonely Planet World Guide: Azerbaijan. www.lonelyplanet.com/worldguide/destinations/europe/azerbaijan

The Library of Congress Country Studies: Azerbaijan. http://lcweb2.loc.gov/frd/cs/aztoc.html

Welcome to Baku. www.baku.com

MUSIC

Anthology of World Music: Azerbaijan. Various artists. Rounder Select, 2003.

Azerbaijan: Songs of the Greater Caucasus. Various artists. Buda Musique, 2002.

Aziza. Aziza Mustafa Zadeh. Sony, 1993.

Fikret Amirov: Shur-Azerbaijan Mugam No. 1; Azerbaijan Capriccio. Fikret Amirov. World Asv Living, 1998.

Legendary Art of Mugham. Alim Qasimov. World Network, 1998.

Love's Deep Ocean. Alim Qasimov. World Network, 2000.

BIBLIOGRAPHY

Altstadt, Audrey L. *The Azerbaijan Turks: Power and Identity under Russian Rule*. Palo Alto, CA: Hoover Institution Press, 1992.

Curtis, Glenn E., ed. *Armenia, Azerbaijan and Georgia*. Washington, D.C.: Library of Congress, 1995.

Plunkett, Richard, and Tom Masters. *Georgia, Armenia and Azerbaijan*. Victoria, Australia: Lonely Planet Publications, 2004.

Swietochowski, Tadeusz. *Historical Dictionary of Azerbaijan*. Lanham, MD: Scarecrow, 1999.

INDEX

143